LIFE IS SHORT

Life Is Short

AN APPROPRIATELY BRIEF GUIDE TO
MAKING IT MORE MEANINGFUL

DEAN RICKLES

PRINCETON UNIVERSITY PRESS

PRINCETON & OXFORD

Published by Princeton University Press
41 William Street, Princeton, New Jersey 08540
99 Banbury Road, Oxford OX2 6JX

press.princeton.edu

All Rights Reserved

Library of Congress Cataloging-in-Publication Data

Names: Rickles, Dean, author.
Title: Life is short : an appropriately brief guide to making it more
    meaningful / Dean Rickles.
Description: Princeton : Princeton University Press, [2022] | Includes
    bibliographical references and index.
Identifiers: LCCN 2022013109 (print) | LCCN 2022013110 (ebook) |
    ISBN 9780691240596 (acid-free paper) | ISBN 9780691240602 (ebook)
Subjects: LCSH: Seneca, Lucius Annaeus, approximately
    4 B.C.-65 A.D. De brevitate vitae. | Life. | Time management. |
    BISAC: PHILOSOPHY / General | SELF-HELP / Death,
    Grief, Bereavement
Classification: LCC B616.D43 R53 2022 (print) | LCC B616.D43 (ebook) |
    DDC 128/.4—dc23/eng/20220512
LC record available at https://lccn.loc.gov/2022013109
LC ebook record available at https://lccn.loc.gov/2022013110

British Library Cataloging-in-Publication Data is available

Editorial: Rob Tempio and Chloe Coy
Production Editorial: Natalie Baan
Jacket Design: Karl Spurzem
Production: Erin Suydam
Publicity: Carmen Jimenez and Alyssa Sanford
Copyeditor: Hank Southgate

Jacket image: pink rose © Quang Ho / Shutterstock

This book has been composed in Arno

Printed on acid-free paper. ∞

Printed in the United States of America

10 9 8 7 6 5 4 3 2 1

To La Belginqué

"Well," said the witch, "I know everything that's going to happen to you." Then she remarked that Dominic was unusually wise for so young a dog and offered him a bit of information. "I hope you don't mind if I tell you this much," she said. "That road there on the right goes nowhere. There's not a bit of magic up that road, no adventure, no surprise, nothing to discover or wonder at. Even the scenery is humdrum. You'd soon grow much too introspective. You'd take to daydreaming and tail-twiddling, get absent-minded and lazy, forget where you are and what you're about, sleep more than one should, and be wretchedly bored. Furthermore, after a while, you'd reach a dead end and you'd have to come all that dreary way back to right here where we're standing now, only it wouldn't be now, it would be some woefully wasted time later."

—WILLIAM STEIG, DOMINIC[1]

CONTENTS

Preface xi

Acknowledgments xv

1   The Shortness of Life, Redux   1

2   Who Wants to Live Forever?   10

3   People and Purpose   16

4   Diseases of Time   27

5   Project Me   43

6   The Provisional Life   56

7   Bulletproofing   70

8   The Meaning of ~~Life~~ Death   80

Notes 95

Index 113

PREFACE

Limitation. Unlimited possibilities are not suited to man: if they existed, his life would only dissolve in the boundless.

—I CHING, HEXAGRAM 60[1]

WE DISSOLVE INTO the boundless without limits, says the *I Ching*. The present book was conceived just prior to, and written entirely during, the COVID-19 pandemic. We were certainly limited by this in all kinds of ways. Right now I am writing this very sentence during a statewide lockdown, like a prisoner, unable to do more than stroll outside for an hour each day and do some essential shopping.

For many, the pandemic has provided a rare pause to the hustle and bustle of daily life. It is as if the world itself is suffering from a midlife crisis. We have had to drop whatever order was present and create new orders in a bid to preserve sanity. Some cope better than others. Some people's lives barely changed. Others' were turned upside down. Some have realized that they didn't much like how their lives were before, all work and no play, and are reluctant to go back to the old ways. Some have become so terrified by the prospect of death from COVID that they have effectively walled themselves off from life and the risks it entails. In all cases, there is an inter-play between limit and possibility, but also with freedom. We think of limitations (especially death) as things that disrupt our freedom precisely because they remove possibilities. This book argues otherwise. Paradoxically, limit gives birth to freedom.

I take the above passage from the *I Ching* to mean that with no constraints, with no limits, no boundaries or walls—if life were to "reset" to an autosave point as in a computer game—there would be no *meaning* to action. No consequences. How dull are games without rules and consequences? Not a game at all. The game of life must contain boundaries. And a good thing too. While we are seemingly squeezed by our lack of unlim-ited possibilities (i.e., our short lives), an unlimited being is squeezed in other ways: it would simply not have any means to enjoy a meaningful existence as we do. It is an existence as boring as the game with no rules in which there is nothing to act against and nothing to act *for*.

To be a free agent is precisely to be a being who faces con-sequences. To be an agent is to *have* to choose, to decide, from a finite sample. It is to let go of some possibilities in favor of others. To prune the branches of one's future. To let them die or actively kill them off. But to be an agent is to be a creature who can have a meaningful life precisely by virtue of such acts of pruning. To have a good, meaningful life is to have a con-scious, *authentic* life in which actions and aims are aligned and any pruning of branches is done with purpose, rather than ran-domly snapping them or having others prune them for you. To have a meaningful life, death is necessary: death of the dis-carded branches (the possibilities that are lost in favor of what is made actual) and the eventual death of the self.

Death is the most necessary limit of all, and without it, all projects are devalued. Death is the source of meaning since it is the very source of choice, of having to decide. Unlimited time would imply that all possible outcomes could occur at some point, so that choice would not even be a coherent concept—it would simply *dissolve into the boundless*. (Interestingly, critics of the so-called many-worlds interpretation of quantum mechanics—according to which, roughly speaking, every "choice" really involves all possible outcomes and you are simply restricted to one "branch" among many—raise similar issues: if all worlds, covering all possible outcomes for choices are realized, then the very notion of possibilities, of things *happening*, in the sense of *becoming actual*, seems to be rendered meaningless.) Death and the shortness of life naturally occupy us for most of this book. In fact, the book is envisaged as a reassessment of the themes raised by Seneca in his classic work *On the Shortness of Life*.[2] And indeed we find many of Seneca's old concerns are still very much present and push their way into all of the themes of this book.

Death is considered explicitly right at the start, where we lay out Seneca's ideas and dismiss the old Epicurean stance that death is nothing to concern us. We go on to consider the idea of immortality, of removing the future boundary of death, and focus on what that would imply from the point of view of life's meaning. This is also considered from the point of view of a *collective* afterlife and the role, if any, played by the continuation of others after your own death. I bundle other Senecan ideas into the idea of a "disease of time" having to do with our poor decision-making when it comes to our futures (often behaving in ways that might seem to imply we are immortal).

I suggest a way of making sense of this behavior and consider ways of curing this disease by thinking of the future as a kind of sculpture that we impose our will on. This idea, however, faces problems from the need to perform a kind of balancing act between a pair of opposing attitudes (each with temporal elements: present-focused and future-focused, or *Puer* versus *Senex*) that pose problems for would-be sculptors, forcing the carving to manifest in unintended, problematic ways. We push this framework further, considering the problem of what I call "bulletproofing," namely of attempting to make one's sculpture almost too perfect and invulnerable. We end by pulling all of these strands together, showing how they converge onto the idea of a meaningful life, along with the essential requirement that it be a (relatively) short one bookended by birth and death.

This is a short book, as the title says, because time is precious—before you get indignant, I'm not against long books. While some books *need* to be long, it would surely be inappropriate for a book on a topic such as this to take too much time away from your short life. I hope you can transform this small investment into a somewhat improved, somewhat enriched life. A more meaningful life. I hope it makes you think deeply and hard, and differently, about matters of life and death.

ACKNOWLEDGMENTS

THIS PROJECT/RESEARCH was supported by grant number FQXi-RFP-1817 from the Foundational Questions Institute and Fetzer Franklin Fund, a donor advised fund of Silicon Valley Community Foundation as well as a grant [ID# 62106] from the John Templeton Foundation. The opinions expressed in this publication are those of the author and do not necessarily reflect the views of the John Templeton Foundation, the Foundational Questions Institute, or the Fetzer Franklin Fund. It also benefited from an Australian Research Council Discovery Project Grant [DP210100919]. Thanks to my editor at Princeton University Press, Rob Tempio, for putting his faith in this project, as well as sage advice and several examples that appear in the book, including the utterly perfect opening passage from William Steig.

Thank you to Gaia for putting up with much grumpiness and distractedness in the latter stages of writing this book, and thank you to my Mira for her patience and love through the same.

DPR
Berrima, NSW
November 2021

LIFE IS SHORT

1

The Shortness of Life, Redux

Most of humankind, Paulinus, complains about the spitefulness of Nature, on grounds that we're born for a short life span, and that these moments of time that have been given to us dart away so quickly, so swiftly, that only a few escape this pattern: Life deserts us when we're just getting ready for life.

—SENECA, OPENING WORDS OF
ON THE SHORTNESS OF LIFE[1]

LUCIUS ANNAEUS SENECA (Seneca the Younger: circa 4BC–CE65) wrote a beautiful and appropriately brief book called *On the Shortness of Life*. The book you are now reading is in part intended to provide a kind of updating of that classic work, which was really one of the first self-help books.[2]

Seneca was the tutor of the young Nero, who would become Emperor of Rome. In fact, Seneca committed suicide to evade being subject to interrogation over a plot to kill Nero (the so-called Pisonian conspiracy). It was a rather gruesome death. After first slitting his wrists and legs, he failed to properly bleed out. He then took hemlock, but by then his circulation had been reduced, so that failed too. So, he was placed in a warm bath to speed up his circulation.[3] Being entangled with the powerful, Seneca got himself mixed up in various other intrigues: he was exiled, supposedly for having slept with the "Mad Emperor" Caligula's sister (given the gossip about him, Caligula may have been jealous!).

On the Shortness of Life was written around 55 CE. Intrigue was indeed rather commonplace for major public figures then, as it remains, and probably played a role in the writing of the book. Though directed at his father-in-law, Paulinus, purportedly in a bid to have him retire from public life (where he was charged with the administration of Rome's grain supply as *praefectus annonae*), it seems Paulinus was already on the way out (in favor of Agrippina's preferred chap, Faenius Rufus), and the book was more of a face-saving exercise so he could exit without shame. Since it contains many negative remarks about life in the upper echelons of Rome, the book was unlikely to have done Seneca any favors there.

"Seneca" can be translated into English as "old man." Ironic, given his book's title, but also quite apt, since our time, for Seneca, should be viewed as the most valuable commodity there is: the most precious substance in the universe, far transcending material goods. This is certainly not just a case of "time is money": time is infinitely more precious than money, which is fungible and reusable. Of course, time is a peculiar substance, and quite probably no kind of substance at all in the usual sense: we can't see it, or smell it, or hear it. We have no special sense organ for time. We only see processes *in* time, and these processes are sometimes, unfortunately, associated with our aging: the motions of celestial bodies marking out the years, clocks ticking, calendars being turned over, pages in diaries being filled up, and so on.

The sad thing about time, or at least our journey through it, is, of course, that it is seemingly taking place down a one-way street. We can't re-experience old events directly. Only by accessing memories. Hence, we have a key element of its preciousness: every event is *unique*, never to be repeated. As another Roman writer, the Epicurean philosopher Lucretius, puts it in *On the Nature of Things*, "Presently the present will have gone, never to be recalled."[4] If we adopt an economics of value-in-scarcity, then we can see why time is so valuable. One should use this resource most wisely, counsels Seneca, not wasting any of it on frivolous pursuits.[5] And yet that is exactly what most people do: complaining about not having enough time on Earth while squandering it. We should not be bitter at nature, at the universe, for this sorry state of affairs, but at ourselves. We should rather be thankful for what time we have been given. Hence Seneca's view defended in *On the Shortness of Life* that "[i]t's not that we have a short time to live, but that we waste a lot of it."[6]

I'm sure Seneca would be horrified to see how so many people spend so much of it on Facebook, Instagram, and other social media! Years of a "Millennial's" or "Zoomer's" lifespan are spent idling on these platforms, concerned more with how they appear than how they *are*, never giving themselves space to properly think—true even of a good deal of my academic colleagues, I might add! I share Seneca's horror at the great wastage of time—I ditched all social media for this reason, and felt better almost immediately. (Chapter 4 will deal with some of the reasons *why* we have a tendency to waste our time, and then chapter 5 will try and provide some means for combatting it.)

In Seneca's day, the average life expectancy was a mere forty years. Life really was short back then. Though our lifespan, at least in developed Western countries, has doubled, it is still a relatively short life. Looking back at the prolific nature of some short lives way back when, you wouldn't think we've only relatively recently doubled average lifespans. Seneca's message still strikes forcefully home, and I will refer back often to his small book, which still manages to encapsulate mountains of words (and songs!) that came after him.

Yet, with apologies to Seneca, life is still too damn short: I want more, and so, probably, do you, at least if the many supposedly life-extending supplements are anything to go by. Rather than extending life, this book, like Seneca's (whatever its initial motivation might have been), is principally about using your most precious resource, time, wisely and more effectively—and also more consciously, with an awareness of how extraordinary it is that you have any time at all. I want to take as little as possible from you in this book. Time is surely the most curious and ill-understood element in the universe, second only to (and probably profoundly connected to) the mystery of why anything exists at all. Time enables me to return to this same computer in the same room to type more words. It is a superbly efficient way to recycle materials, and indeed my view of time's role in the universe is based on this principle of efficiency (the universe is the great optimizer) and *doing the most with the least*, much as Seneca suggested we ought to do with time itself.

Our lives are of course temporal entities. We might think that the following simple equation holds true: Time = Life. Our life is clearly bookended by times, marking our birth and death. Though as the nineteenth-century German philosopher Hegel rightly noted, birth is essentially a death-sentence:

> The nature of finite things as such is to have the seed of passing away as their essential being: the hour of their birth is the hour of their death.[7]

The mind has its own kind of event horizon too. Just as you are limited by the span of time within which you exist, so you have limited resources at any one, single time within that already limited timespan. Only a small snapshot of reality can be captured by your mind in a moment, lasting roughly a few milliseconds to a few seconds or so. This is your immediate awareness, or what the great psychologist and philosopher William James called "the specious present."[8] This is reality for you. It is your *Now*. Philosophers get all excited about this, because we clearly have to infer the rest of the universe, including the past and future, an external world, and other minds, from this tiny window of present experience. The Austrian musicologist Viktor Zuckerkandl puts it rather well:

> What a precarious situation, balancing on the hairline of the present, which, itself evaporating into immeasurability, separates two oceans of non-being.[9]

Indeed, there are then two kinds of nonbeing we find ourselves wedged between: the past and future that form the boundary of our present and also the prenatal and postdeath nonbeing that form those above-mentioned bookends marking the boundary of our lives (at least, it is nonbeing as far as *we* are concerned).

But according to Seneca, the equation "Time = Life" is not quite right. Simply existing (or enduring) time is not the same as living: "all the rest of existence is not life, but merely time."[10] The Latin word for life, *vitae*, brings up this difference. Life is vital. As he writes,

> There's no reason to think someone's lived long, on account of their grey hair and wrinkles. That person only existed, not lived, a long time. Would you say that a man has done much voyaging, if, as soon as he left port, a violent storm seized him and, with furious blasts of wind arising from every direction, drove him in a circle over the same route? He didn't do much journeying, he was only much tossed around.[11]

Long or short, we surely want a journey. Adding up the time actually lived—really *lived*—we often have a short life indeed, but only because so much time was spent unlived, often in a kind of limbo, waiting for life to happen to us (a topic we return to in chapter 6, when we consider the notion of "the provisional life"). Rather than making life happen, we choose to view through our tiny window of presentness quite unworthy contents.

To have a good journey, we often need a good map. Seneca wanted to provide such a map. A way of not going off course. A way to avoid too many distractions and wrong turns. Seneca was a classic example of a Stoic philosopher who often wrote guides to *good living*. We now think of "stoic" as a term referring to a person who suffers the slings and arrows of outrageous fortune with dignity and equanimity—incidentally, the word "stoic" itself simply comes from the Greek word for porch (*stoa*) under which these philosophers did their philosophizing. The Stoics were a group of philosophers largely associated with such a view of life, but their views are far wider and provided a fairly complete worldview, covering fields as far apart as politics and physics.

I don't wish to make this a book on Stoicism, which seems to have become something of a fad of late, most likely as a corrective to the anxiety and narcissism epidemic seemingly coursing through society, but also, no doubt, as a nontoxic corrective to the attacks on so-called toxic masculinity. But I do briefly want to switch to another, rather more famous Greek philosopher, Epicurus, who was also concerned with matters of life and death—though more so with easing anxiety over the shortness of life, rather than debating whether it really is all that short or how to fill it up.

Death anxiety is of course very common—I have it in spades.[12] As Jean-Jacques Rousseau once put it,

> He who pretends to look on death without fear lies. All men are afraid of dying, this is the great law of sentient beings, without which the entire human species would soon be destroyed.[13]

Yet Epicurus famously said, "Death is nothing to us." Why? Because of a simple argument: "When we exist, death is not; and when death exists, we are not."[14] Now, of course, a dead person will not suffer. Indeed, the phrase "dead person" might be viewed as an oxymoron: a person must be alive and kicking to be a person. Being dead is not really a *state* of a person in the sense of your home being tidy. But what about the process of going from *living* to *dying* to *dead*? Here one is losing the property of being alive. That might be something we don't wish to lose, even though once lost there is no self left to care about it!

Lucretius, the Epicurean philosopher mentioned above, presented another better-known version of this argument against death terror, based on a symmetry between the two states of nonbeing (prenatal and postmortem) mentioned above:

> Look back at the time before one's birth. In this way, Nature holds before our eyes a mirror of our future after death. Is this so grim, or so gloomy?[15]

In other words, you don't worry about not existing in the period *before* you were born, and yet that is qualitatively no different (a mirror image) to the kind of nonexistence that will occur *after* you are dead. We should surely treat symmetrical situations in the same way if we want to be rational beings, so if we do not worry about our past nonexistence, then neither should we worry about our future nonexistence.

There are many ways we can face this argument. The French novelist Michel Houellebecq once pointed out in an interview that the symmetry argument doesn't work when considering other people.[16] That is, it might work perfectly well when considering your own death, but not the death of a loved one. We can say a similar things about Epicurus's no-harm argument: death might not harm the dead, but it can certainly harm those left behind.

This is all perfectly true, but let us be selfish and keep the focus on ourselves here—don't worry, we will pay penance for this later in discussions of narcissism. Does the symmetry argument help us? I don't think so. To say as the Epicureans do that death is nothing to worry about is to ignore its indispensable role in providing meaning through the enforcing of choices. Death is crucial to meaning because it provides a finite boundary, and that is really a key point of this book. Death should not be dismissed so lightly: it should be seen more as the gift that breathes life into existence and gives existence a point.

Much of this has to do with a fairly basic feature of time that we have already mentioned, namely that time goes in one direction, and as it does it seals off past events from further influence. This has all kinds of implications that are significant for humans. As Herman Melville puts it in his novel *White-Jacket*, "The Past is dead, and has no resurrection; but the Future is endowed with such a life, that it lives to us even in anticipation."[17] In other words, the arrow of time points to the fact that the premises of the symmetry argument are incorrect: the past and the future are not to be treated in the same way when it comes to the human scale since one way is open to possibilities and the other is closed. The next chapter deals with what would happen when we have no constraints on such future possibilities.

2

Who Wants to Live Forever?

"Too bad you can only live so long."
—VITEK, IN LEOŠ JANÁČEK'S *VĔC MAKROPULOS*[1]

THE PREVIOUS CHAPTER's idea of the source of our death anxiety as having to do with the closing off of ever more possibilities in the future (an open future) is itself the source of so many of our fantasies of immortality: the prospect of many more possible experiences. There is a kind of FOMO (i.e., "fear of missing out") on a grand, terminal scale here: death anxiety is the ultimate FOMO. Indeed, we might, as the English poet Philip Larkin famously put it, see religion (that "vast moth-eaten musical brocade") as simply a way of "pretending we never die" to try to alleviate some of this anxiety.[2]

The Czech author Karel Čapek wrote a play titled *Vĕc Makropulos* (*The Makropulos Case*), later turned into an opera by Leoš Janáček, from which this chapter's opening quote was taken. This tells of Elina Makropulos, who was made effectively immortal through a potion developed by a court alchemist for her father, Emperor Rudolf II. Eventually, as the potion loses its effect, at the age of 342—it has a 300-year efficacy, though more can be made from the alchemical formula to extend life indefinitely through these 300-year shots—she decides to allow death to take her. Her rationale: for meaning and purpose, there must also be death, an absolute limit to one's possibilities. So, to return to the theme of Seneca, the verdict of Makropulos is that life is not so very short after all: it is more or less the length it needs to be to hold together in a meaningful way.

I will admit that 342 years seems unnecessarily brief to me—even my own personal library would not be read through by then, and I doubt I could master all the languages, musical instruments, mathematics, interesting skills (unicycling, juggling very many balls, solving Rubik's Cubes at high speed, etc.), that I would like to by then. There would no doubt be great variation in our preferred "jumping off" points, having to do with our personalities—and, likely, levels of self-absorption. Indeed, I imagine one could learn much about the personalities of individuals by asking them how long they would like to live and what they would do with that time.

The philosopher Sir Bernard Williams utilized this story to great effect in his paper "The Makropulos Case: Reflections on the Tedium of Immortality."[3] But I think tedium as such is the wrong aspect to focus on. Indeed, many have responded to Williams that there seem to be a great many substances from which we do not seem to suffer from diminishing returns: love springs to mind. Or, more concretely perhaps, heroin addicts don't seem to get bored of taking it, though of course they require more and more to attain the same state, and so the effects diminish in that sense. Williams clearly envisages the space of our desires as something like a chessboard with a large but finite number of possibilities, all of which we will eventually actualize and eventually duplicate over and over again in the style of Nietzsche's eternal return.[4] This is not necessarily true, and there is no strong reason to believe that this is how reality is put together instead of an unending sea of possibilities.

One might wonder, however, whether it is even coherent to speak of immortality for humans like us. As Williams points out, we must demand that there is a self who endures throughout this eternity; otherwise there is no thing that is immortal, but instead just a sequence of distinct things. Yet, as the Scottish Enlightenment philosopher Thomas Reid argued— against English philosopher and physician John Locke's memory (and psychological continuity or sameness of consciousness) theory of the identity of the self over time—it is often difficult to speak of an enduring self even in perfectly ordinary (mortal) scenarios.[5]

Consider Reid's own example of an eighty-year-old army general. As a forty-year-old officer, he might be able to remember his experiences as a boy of ten, scrumping apples. Likewise, the old general might remember his days as that officer of forty, but still not, at that late time of life, remember scrumping apples as a boy.[6] This kind of example brings out some of the problems with supposing that humans like us could be immortal in any meaningful sense. Even if we consider extending lifespans to one thousand years, let alone eternity, if we are assuming we are dealing with the ordinary human memory system, we must consider problems with making sense of the existence of an enduring self over such long times. Indeed, it seems as if our life-spans are more or less set up to match our long-term memory capacities: just about capacious enough to fit an entire, unified life (assuming that one does not have the misfortune to be afflicted with Alzheimer's disease).

Of course, we are speculating wildly here. Who knows what "life" would be like if we were actually immortal? It is, for example, surely inconceivable that with eternity at our disposal we would not modify our living conditions and possibly our own bodies in such a way that the resulting beings would be wholly unrecognizable. But we can at least speculate from what we know about the lives we do have, and if we do so, what we find is that the immortal life, though perhaps exhibiting moment-to-moment continuity, would be akin to a series of lives, separated by an inability to remember—much like the past-lives phenomenon, in which people claim to have glimpses of old events when they inhabited a different body (usually some famous figure, naturally). Curiously, this is almost exactly how Plato (e.g., in his dialogue *Phaedo*, concerning the transmigration of the soul, or *metempsychosis*) and other reincarnationists conceive of the immortal soul. However, the selfsame problem we discussed above can simply be raised here: how are we to even think of these "reborn" selves as one and the same enduring individual if they lack knowledge of such endurance through the various rebirths?[7]

Immortality aside, just how far are we from reaching even 342 years of age with modern alchemy? The oldest person to have ever lived without any such life-prolonging, medical interventions was 122 when she died—a French woman named Jeanne Louise Calment, who died in 1997. The English gerontologist Aubrey de Grey famously proposed a set of "Strategies for Engineered Negligible Senescence" (SENS) (yes, it is a pun on the root of the word Seneca). The idea is to find mechanisms of aging and then to intervene in those mechanisms. As with a car mechanic, we would simply go for a tune-up when we needed to prolong our lives. He writes, "[We] are machines, and aging is the wearing out of a machine, the accumulation of damage to a machine, and hence potentially fixable."[8] So far there is much talk (e.g., lengthening of telomeres[9]), and though some of the basic ideas are sound, there are no significant practical outcomes yet, and Jeanne Louise Calment's record appears safe. However, de Grey's proposals (like many related so-called bio-hacking ideas) relate to a topic we turn to later: the eternal youth (or "*puer aeternis*") phenomenon and the folly of pursuing such an idea too forcefully—the *puer aeternis* chafes at being limited in any way and seeks Godlike perfection.

Indeed, de Grey himself is very much an example of a *puer aeternis*, speaking glowingly of the idea of "indefinite youth" and of "curing aging" as if it were some terrible disease.[10] There is in this a desire to be unbounded. The intuitions of immortalists like de Grey are clearly in direct opposition to finitists like Williams, the latter writing in stark contrast that if immortal "I would eventually have had altogether too much of myself."[11]

Alas, until the de Greys of the world manage to appreciably extend our lifespans, which is entirely possible, we are left speculating on the shortness of our lives, and still apparently unable to stop ourselves from misusing this all too brief time. We turn to this scandalous misuse in chapter 4. Before we get to that, I would first like to discuss a different kind of immortality, involving the people who will keep humanity going after our still-inevitable deaths. The purpose of this apparent detour is to make some headway on the links between mortality (and time in a rather loose sense) and meaning, for there has been some recent philosophical work claiming to show that in fact some kind of afterlife (at least of other people existing after our deaths) is a necessary condition for a meaningful life. If, as I argue in this book, the shortness of life is required for a meaningful life, then why do we have this apparent conflict arising at the collective level? We show how this conflict can in fact be dissolved.

3

People and Purpose

A world which has no people in it is pointless. A universe that is just chugging away by itself with nobody in it is, in a sense, pointless.

—INTERVIEW WITH ROGER PENROSE[1]

IT IS QUITE COMMON these days, with various anthropogenic calamities befalling us, to wish an end to people, to humanity as a whole, to allow the Earth to recover. On this planet, we're like "a virus in shoes," as the American comedian Bill Hicks once put it.[2] We've seen how the coronavirus lockdowns almost immediately led to a rebound in the quality of the natural environment. Alan Weisman predicted some of this long ago in his book *The World without Us*,[3] arguing that nature would take over the day after humans disappear—the silent assumption being, of course, that we are somehow *not* nature.

And indeed it is entirely conceivable that we might perish in a catastrophic event.[4] The global climate shifts might easily render the planet uninhabitable, especially in combination with explosive population growth—"I think we're fucked," as former Microsoft chief scientist Stephen Emmott so eloquently puts it at the close of his book *Ten Billion*.[5]

You can find such antihuman sentiments expressed in particularly stark form in the so-called Voluntary Human Extinction Movement.[6] The idea, due to Les Knight (appropriately vasectomized, I'm happy to report), is that humans are so bad that we ought to be phased out of this universe. The ideas were triggered by Paul and Anne Ehrlich's neo-Malthusian (and, quite frankly, borderline Doomsday cult) book, *The Population Bomb*,[7] which scared many people into activism, the consequences of which we are witnessing today.

But now suppose you learned that all humans from now on will indeed stop having children. The Voluntary Human Extinctionists among you would no doubt be thrilled. But how would that affect the remainder of your life? Knowing that yours is the last "batch" of humans, would your actions, your *striving*, still even make sense? In philosopher Samuel Scheffler's terminology, this would be taking away "the afterlife."[8] Not afterlife in any religious sense, but simply in the sense of there being life (human life other than your own) that continues after your own death. This scenario involves, then, the shortness of *collective* human life. This is a great intuition pump, and we can play with it a little to get a grip on some key concepts.

The example Scheffler gives, of afterlife elimination, involves an armageddon-style scenario, only this time with no bestubbled Bruce Willis to save the day. We know that just one month after your death (it's OK: you die of natural causes), the Earth will be hit by a gigantic meteor, thereby obliterating all of humanity. Assume this is certain. The question is, would it change anything about how you live? Would you give up, or carry on as before? Would your behavior relative to the others in this ultimate cohort alter? If so, why? What is it about the presence of others (those who will exist *after* you die) that makes a difference to the meaning of your own life? It seems to most that Penrose is right: without this kind of afterlife, without human beings, the universe becomes a pointless place.

Scheffler himself uses his thought experiment to demonstrate that our lives gain much of their meaning from an unexpressed belief in a "collective afterlife" that will keep the world going, seemingly in contrast to the idea we expressed (and will defend further) that it is its very shortness that gives a life its meaning. The thought that such an afterlife might not exist troubles people. It troubles them that the human world would stop, despite the indifferent continuation of everything else. That nobody would read and write books—even short ones like this. Or compose music. Or make art. Or bake cakes. Or play Scrabble. Or walk in the countryside. Drink red wine. This is not just a case of being troubled by these other lives ending per se. It is something else.

In fact, the example can easily be modified so that no one dies untimely deaths, in a great tragedy, but instead their numbers just dwindle to zero, much as the Voluntary Human Extinction Movement would like if they had their way. Here Scheffler draws from P. D. James's dystopian novel *The Children of Men*, in which reproductive issues point to a complete extinction of humans within a century.[9] Deaths are natural until then, and lives are fully lived out. But Scheffler points out, rightly I think, that we would still be troubled here too. It is the very *absence* of humanity itself that troubles, not how that absence arose. It seems to remove the ground from all kinds of endeavors. Why would I write this book, for example, if it became clear that there would be no human left to read it once it was completed? Hopefully I'm not being too ambitious to think that at least one person might read it!

We can push in several ways on this example. One is the temporal horizon for the extinction event. Thirty days after your death is very close. Not much would have changed in the world. But we all know that things cannot last forever in this universe, what with its relentless entropic decline. We know we are governed, for example, by a supermassive black hole sitting at the center of our galaxy, the Milky Way, which will eventually suck everything in, eradicating all record of humanity. There really is no afterlife if we we consider "after" to be sufficiently far into the future. At some point, we really are fucked, along with the other complex structures in the universe. In this case, we are able to perform the appropriate cognitive dissonance to pretend nothing's the matter. But we might find that there is in fact a kind of irrationality in treating the thirty-day extinction as any different from, say, the seven to eight billion years until the death of our Sun, spelling humanity's doom (or doom for whatever comes after us). If it ends, why should it matter when, so long as you get to live out a normal life? After all, even all traces of those people who will continue to exist for a long time after your death will eventually be wiped out too at some point.

Scheffler in fact brings in the following wonderful scene from Woody Allen's *Annie Hall*[10] on this point, where we have a young, depressed Alvy Singer (= young Woody, neurotic as ever):

DR. FLICKER: Why are you depressed, Alvy?

ALVY'S MOTHER: Tell Dr. Flicker. (*Alvy sits hunched; whereupon his mother answers.*)

ALVY'S MOTHER: It's something he read.

DR. FLICKER: Something he read, huh?

ALVY: (*His head still down.*) The universe is expanding.

DR. FLICKER: The universe is expanding?

ALVY: Well, the universe is everything, and if it's expanding, someday it will break apart and that would be the end of everything!

ALVY'S MOTHER: Why is that your business? (*She turns back to the doctor.*) He stopped doing his homework!

ALVY: What's the point?

ALVY'S MOTHER: What has the universe got to do with it? You're here in Brooklyn! Brooklyn is not expanding.

DR. FLICKER: It won't be expanding for billions of years yet, Alvy. We've gotta try to enjoy ourselves while we're here!

Scheffler insists that Alvy is being silly because of the time scales involved: billions of years versus thirty years. If the numbers were reversed, Alvy would be right to be depressed, and we'd be back to the *Children of Men* scenario. But my intuitions differ here, and I suspect that it is a disease of time (the human bias for present and near-future events—on which you must await the next chapter) that is feeding Scheffler's intuitions that I fail to share.

Another way to push on the intuition is to consider something like the Lucretian symmetry argument we mentioned in chapter 1 as a way to ease death anxiety. If it is indeed an absence of humanity that troubles us, then why are we not troubled by that absence in earlier times? There is a large "humanless chasm" stretching between the Big Bang and the first, conscious, self-aware human. Again, this example reveals that time (specifically the arrow of time in this example) is playing a crucial role, for it is the forward nature of our projects that matters. We know that we can influence the future but not the past.

So, ultimately at least, there is perhaps no afterlife—though this can't be ruled out, of course, and we may possess an immortal soul. There's perhaps also no God of the Bible, if we believe Nietzsche (see below)—though some kind of creative intelligence can't be ruled out either. Regardless, there's certainly no agreed-upon explanation for the universe's existence, for why it is even here at all. How will you live then? In a brief yet profound talk, "Is Life Worth Living?," William James considered exactly such issues (focusing on suicide), arguing that we really require an "unseen order" (or an assumption that such a thing exists) for it all to make sense.[11] James's unseen order aside, if there is no reason for the universe's being here (and so far as we can tell, there isn't: James himself suggests we simply have the "right to believe" that there is some spiritual order grounding reality in a good foundation), then why bother going on at all?

Philosopher Thomas Nagel called this fact of going on in an apparently meaningless universe an "absurdity."[12] That is, there is great irony in the seriousness with which we take our lives and projects given that they have no ultimate meaning or ground in the world. There is no justification for anything we do, because that would require something *beyond* itself (that unseen order James urges us to accept as an axiom of nonsuicidality). The philosopher-novelist Albert Camus referred more poetically to "the confrontation between the human need" (with its "wild longing for clarity") and "the unreasonable silence of the world."[13] For Nietzsche, of course, this was simply the inescapable condition given the death of God, leaving us abandoned in a meaning vacuum.[14] We really have no grip on why the universe is here at all. It is irrational. It might all be snuffed out in the next instant for all we know. And yet we go on, carving whatever meaning we can into this silent world. Of course, this leads many to nihilism or hedonism: if there's no sense or meaning in the world, then why live in any other way than doing just what feels right to you? This is certainly rampant in the world right now—I provide an alternative to nihilism in the subsequent chapters.

Phrased in these terms, this all seems to be pretty much covering old existentialist ground, only with a shiny new vehicle. In the older existentialism, of Sartre and company, the problem was how to make meaning in a world in which God is dead and there is no reason for the existence of the world. No rule book of any kind. Their answer was that we need to make our own. We have no essential nature drawn from the world of things: "existence precedes essence" is the motto.[15] Now, with Scheffler's idea, we are faced with a different kind of answer: we don't need God, but we do need the larger collective provided by ongoing Humanity.

But there might be something else going on here, which has more to do with a desire to have things *preserved*. It might simply be latent conservatism. One finds this in something so simple as a sandcastle. We build a grand structure on the beach, lovingly carving moats and so on, and we would like it to continue. We get rather disappointed when it is taken by the sea or, worse, is destroyed by other beachgoers. Is it then the existence of a collective afterlife that is primary here, or what *function* that collective performs in preserving the sandcastles of civilization from the inevitable entropy? It is quite possible that the work is being done by the order the collective afterlife provides as an antidote to entropy. We are after all beings who love order. This would be more about our own ego than the lives of the others per se. In any case, I don't think this is so straightforward. Intuitions diverge. I don't think we can agree so quickly with Scheffler in his thinking that such scenarios reveal "the limits of egoism."[16]

My own view of the role of humanity in the universe aligns more closely with that of English polymath Roger Penrose, as expressed in the opening quote of this chapter—the final chapter will discuss this view further. Penrose, joint winner of the 2020 Nobel Prize in Physics for his contributions to the theory of gravitation and black holes, comes from a rather illustrious and interesting family. His father, Lionel, was a famous eugenicist involved in changing the subject into "human genetics," distinguishing it from its unsavory past—for example, he was the man behind the changing of the name "mongolism" to "Down's syndrome." Together, Lionel and Roger created the "impossible objects" used by Dutch artist M. C. Escher in his *Ascending and Descending* (fig. 3.1), in which one appears to be able to climb up or down to infinity on a finite, stationary image (the Penrose staircase), as well as the "impossible triangle," used by Escher in his *Waterfall.*[17] This interplay of the finite and the infinite, and especially the idea of bringing infinity into human grasp (into something with a finite boundary so that one can grasp the infinite in the finite), is characteristic of

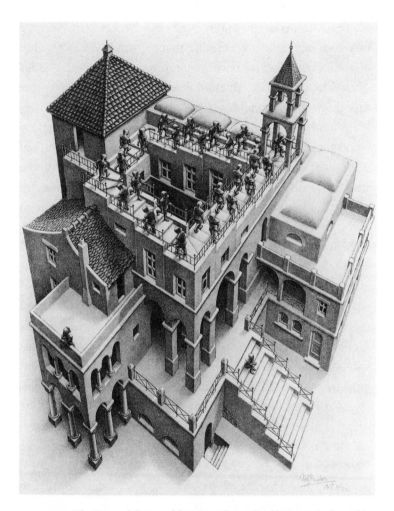

FIGURE 3.1. The Penrose's "impossible staircase" as realized by M. C. Escher in his *Ascending and Descending,* encapsulating the idea of an infinite journey in a finite image. (M. C. Escher's "Ascending and Descending" © 2021 The M. C. Escher Company–The Netherlands. All rights reserved. www.mcescher.com.)

most of Penrose's work, and I like to think of the relationship between death (finitude) and meaning (with its limitlessness) in a similar way.

Penrose views the human mind, or consciousness, as something very special, and it seems to be related again to the same transcendent nature of meaning, which is the mark of the mental: truly the light of the world. Indeed, he has argued that artificial intelligence is impossible since the brain performs in a way that cannot be matched by computational processes: computers could simply never do what we do.[18] In terms of their role in the universe, minds of a certain kind (a *self-aware* kind) are indeed required for a world of meaning. We need selves (subjects) that can *reflect* the world back to itself (as an object). In this case, if we want a meaningful world in the future, then we had better hope there will remain humans (or an "afterlife" with at least something broadly possessing our key characteristics) to provide it. The continued existence does not matter so much for our endeavors in themselves, but more generally for the universe itself to be a meaningful entity.

Penrose's own view of the universe's far future is that eventually everything becomes photons (particles of light). This looks a little like Alvy's nightmare future, but the interesting thing about photons is that they are massless, which means that they do not experience time (this is an effect of Einstein's special theory of relativity), and in a sense (also having to do with their masslessness) neither do they know how big they are. Using this pair of ideas, Penrose thinks that the end of the universe could mark the beginning of another "cycle of time," with another Big Bang, since we can view all the photons as extremely small, forming a new singularity.[19]

The cyclic nature of time expressed here is archetypal: we find it across various cultures, embedded in myths and creation stories. We already mentioned Nietzsche's version of it to test the quality of one's life: would you be OK living your life over and over for all eternity? One might think this leads to a futile existence—a kind of immortality but of a more absurd kind. In his book *Being and Time*,[20] Martin Heidegger also suggests that the meaning of our being must be tied up with time. We are temporal beings, born into a world that existed before us with its religion and culture (something corresponding to a "beforelife"), its history already written, and to make sense of this world, we engage in various pastimes to get by. We might have a family, build a career or a house, and in doing so, we place ourselves on a trajectory toward some sort of future. But there's a limit to our projects, a point at which everything comes to an end, whether finished or unfinished, and that limit is of course our death. This is what Heidegger calls "being-towards-death."[21] However, we are so absorbed by our pastimes and distractions that we simply forget that there's an outermost limit to our pursuits, and in so doing, says Heidegger, we live an inauthentic life. It's not until we project our lives onto the horizon of our death that authentic life can be found[22]—I leave it to you to consider whether the cushion provided by collective immortality in Scheffler's sense also must be transcended. The next chapter deals with another aspect of inauthenticity, more closely related to the wastage of time raised by Seneca, namely our tendency to not do what is in our best, rational interests.

4

Diseases of Time

Truly, though our element is time,
We are not suited to the long perspectives.
—PHILIP LARKIN, "REFERENCE BACK"[1]

HUMANS, AND MOST likely animals in general, suffer from what I call "diseases of time." A disease of time is some behavior relating to the identity of your self over time (i.e., how you feel related to your past and future selves) that leads to negative outcomes. For example, you will be nicer or nastier to your future self depending on the degree of connectedness you feel toward them. It's no different from your treatment of other people depending on your degree of connectedness to them: in general, we are better to our kin than to strangers.[2] We are kin-biased.

In general, faced with someone needing medical attention right in front of you, bleeding before your very eyes, you no doubt would help. But there's plenty of needy, worthy cases scattered across the world, plenty of people in dire need who must suffer only because they happen not to be that person close by. We are proximity-biased.

Distance apparently matters in practice, whether or not it is rational. Temporal distance is no different. We are indeed not suited to long perspectives. We have a nearness-bias with respect to time. We are, in general, better to our present-selves, or five-seconds-into-the-future selves, than we are to our five-years-into-the-future selves. Indeed, we might be said to have yet another kind of temporal event-horizon, a boundary, beyond which we do not show any care to our future self at all: the whole business simply becomes too abstract to act as a guide to action. There are fairly significant individual differences among humans as to where this event horizon lies, but to some extent, the horizon's existence is fairly well-motivated by the difficulty of seeing a clear future through all of the uncertainties that life inevitably throws up.

At an individual level (concerning a person), this temporal myopia obviously can lead to serious problems, e.g., in terms of overeating, overspending, substance abuse, and a whole host of risky behaviors that give a reward right now, or in the immediate future, but a negative outcome further downstream (e.g., obesity, poverty, addictions, unwanted pregnancies, and so on). The disconnectedness prevents individuals from seeing that the future self on the receiving end is still them, and that they have actively created the dire consequences with their present actions. They are the architects of their own suffering.

At the collective level, such behaviors have led to the climate and population crises, with preference given to short-term gains (cheaper and easier fuels, for example) over the health of future people (even if we are included in this poorer future). Some of these global problems are simply upward consequences of various poor individual actions (such as not being bothered to recycle or use birth control).

The problem as it appears in economic behavior is about the distribution of goods over time, where you can think about those goods (maybe how one is paid some amount of money, or how much cake one eats throughout the week) coming to you at those chosen times according to your selection (e.g., a lump sum versus installments). We are bad at doing the right thing when it comes to such matters. We seem to have an inbuilt tendency to choose unhappiness. Think of it this way: We have certain resources, such as time, money, energy, and so on. We face a puzzle about how to spread these about over time (i.e., over our life-span)—a scarce and very precious resource as discussed earlier:

- Should I relax now and do some difficult work task later?
- Should I watch a monkey riding backwards on a pig on YouTube now or do some homework or preparation for a talk?[3]
- Should I stop smoking now or enjoy the buzz it gives me?
- Should I exercise now or just chill out on the sofa?
- Should I eat more greens or have this chocolate?

This is essentially the same problem Seneca was discussing in *On the Shortness of Life*. It simply amounts to the economic problem of *choice over time*: how should we distribute goods over some interval (in this case, one's life)? Seneca's answer (thereby providing a key to the good life, *eudaimonia*) was not to stack too many tough jobs and unpleasant tasks in one's later years, where one should distribute more rewarding tasks after doing the tough stuff early on.

Seneca, it seems, is most concerned with procrastination, the "thief of time" as it is sometimes called. This is a case of putting off what one knows one really ought to do:

> What could be more foolish than the attitude of those who boast of their foresight? They're burdened and busy in an effort to live better; they adorn life by paying out life. They form their thoughts with a long view in mind, but postponement is the greatest waste of a life: It strips away each day in its turn and steals away what's before us while promising what's ahead. Anticipation is the greatest obstacle to living; it depends on tomorrow while squandering today. You make neat rows of things that are in Fortune's hands while letting drop what's in your own. What are you looking toward? What are you aiming for? Everything that's to come is cloaked in uncertainty. Live right now![4]

However, we need to be careful here: what Seneca is referring to is folks putting pleasures off through being very busily engaged in order that they may be able to live better, leading them to spend life in making ready to live! But this doesn't quite ring true to our modern ears. Stop putting off pleasures, you say, Seneca? Erm, OK. Done. This is a Stoics-only problem, it seems. If things were really like this in Seneca's day, then we have severely fallen behind as a species. What we face in modern times is not an overexertion of the will against present pleasures, but the very opposite. There is a will deficit.

This is in fact a very old subject, stretching back far before Seneca. The Greek philosophers called the phenomenon of weakness of will (of, essentially, choosing to be unhappy in the long run) *akrasia* (literally, from the Greek, an absence of command or control).[5] We can find the idea expressed in Homer, in the form of Odysseus having himself bound to the ship's mast in order to not be tempted by the song of the Sirens. Many of us find that we have to perform similar tactics to make sure we are not led down bad avenues. Involuntary pension funds in which a cut is taken from your pay and directly deposited into a savings account is basically the government lashing you to the mast, to avoid the siren call of spending up too soon, leaving you short in your dotage.[6]

There was a wonderful Oxford philosopher (a pure thinker if ever there was one) named Derek Parfit who spent most of his life dealing with the issue of what we owe to others and to ourselves in terms of moral responsibility. He spent much energy in particular on this issue of future selves, arguing that *connectedness* is precisely what matters:

> My concern for my future may correspond to the degree of connectedness between me now and myself in the future. Connectedness is one of the two relations that give me reasons to be specially concerned about my own future. It can be rational to care less, when one of the grounds for caring will hold to a lesser degree. Since connectedness is nearly always weaker over long periods, I can rationally care less about my further future.[7]

In other words, if connectedness really is what matters, then discounting the future as a result of temporal distance is rational after all. Parfit writes of a young boy who takes up smoking, knowing yet not caring that this may cause him to suffer greatly fifty years later. As he points out, the boy does not identify with his future self, treating him as a stranger. Yet, if viewed in these terms, then why not smoke? This should strike you as weird. A person usually cares about what happens in their future life because it is *their* life, not some stranger's.

Perhaps we should simply stop speaking of past and future selves, in favor of simply saying "me." Even "future me" is better than "my future self," which implies a separate existence: multiplicity rather than unity. Parfit's very way of expressing the problem, like many others, involves a conception of multiple selves, overlapping with varying degrees of connectedness, sometimes minimal enough to suggest competition. This is precisely at the root of the larger problems of society, and it does no good to future generations (including those that are not our own future selves) to not promote a healthy interest in our own futures, accepting the disconnection as a fait accompli.

However, what he is saying in terms of our viewing our futures like strangers is perfectly true. Indeed, there have been many empirical studies that seem to corroborate Parfit's idea. Social psychologist Hal Hershfield has used fMRI neural imaging techniques to see what goes on in the brain when one makes "self" versus "other" judgements.[8] One finds the same patterns of activation where strangers and (far) future selves are compared with thinking of one's present self. Parfit suggests that we should take this to mean that strangers ought to be accorded more significance in our lives. I believe, however, that we need to come up with strategies to accord greater significance to our own futures. In other words, I view it as a *problem* that we view our future selves the same way we view strangers (pointing to the need for ways of increasing such a feeling of connectedness), while Parfit views it as the foundation of an ethical viewpoint:

> When I believed [that personal identity is what matters], I seemed imprisoned in myself. My life seemed like a glass tunnel, through which I was moving faster every year, and at the end of which there was darkness. When I changed my view, the walls of my glass tunnel disappeared. I now live in the open air. There is still a difference between my life and the lives of other people. But the difference is less. Other people are closer. I am less concerned about the rest of my own life, and more concerned about the lives of others. When I believed [that personal identity is what matters], I also cared more about my inevitable death. After my death, there will be no one living who will be me. I can now redescribe this fact. Though there will later be many experiences, none of these experiences will be connected to my present experiences by chains of such direct connections as those involved in experience-memory, or in the carrying out of an earlier intention.[9]

This is something akin to Scheffler's afterlife. If my connectedness to my future self is just one among many, then it is no big deal when that one is severed. Again: this strikes me as a bad way to think. It is too *helpless*; the notion of a "glass tunnel" highlights the kind of view of time that Parfit holds, which is that one is not an active participant in one's future, and therefore in the future of the universe itself.

This idea that we are unkind to or unable to care about our future selves the more distant that future is also forms a core part of economic theory, where it is called "temporal (or delay) discounting": humans have a marked tendency to discount the future, and the way they do so follows quite universal laws. In the jargon, we discount "hyperbolically" (so that the graph of the weight given to events drops like a hyperbolic curve as the delay to the event increases). A classic example among academics like myself is agreeing to all manner of projects that are far in the future, only to find themselves swamped when that time finally comes. We don't care *now* about the awful experience that future version of ourselves will have. However, older academics (some of them . . .) learn from their mistakes, and will, if they are smart, store their previous terrible experiences and remember not to say Yes to so many things. This kind of management (temporal economics) ought to be taught early on because school children are particularly prone to leaving their work to the last minute in order to enjoy some more immediate pleasurable event, like doing nothing at all! Parfit's view might well be noble, but it does nothing to help with situations like this.

If one had a more direct view of the future one is creating by the choices one is making now, one would no doubt act very differently. If our actions nonlocally created the future at this very moment, then we remove the relevance of distance: distance doesn't matter so much because we have something acting instantaneously at a distance, like gravity as it was conceptualized in Newton's day, or perhaps in the same way that an engineer might control a robot at a remote site. Interestingly, the physicist David Bohm, famous outside of physics circles for his audiences with the Dalai Lama and Jiddu Krisnamurti, suggested something similar relating to other people too: division into parts (distinct people, distinct selves) is the problem. If we comprise one undivided whole, then they are us, so any bad we do to them is doing bad to ourselves, just as with future selves. This might be going a bit far for some readers, despite Bohm's eminence as a physicist, so let us try to be more concrete.[10]

Quite simply: if one actually saw how eating healthily would create a slimmer, happier, more active future you, then you would be far more likely to eat healthily right now. It is the *deferment* of the outcome that is the problem, the delay in gratification (the slimmer, happier you). There is always a temporal gap, during which we can only reach the outcome by evolving our self through this gap. There is no shortcut. It is a process. You would not perform any of the actions with bad consequences if they were immediate: if you got instant lung disease, or instant tooth decay, and so on. Of course, even one evening is a long enough time horizon not to stop us drinking too heavily, though the process of drinking alcohol eats away at our willpower too. What we need is our own personal Jules-Verne-o-scopes capable of giving us a direct WYSIWYG ("what you see is what you get") display of our futures and the way in which present actions alter this image of the future. Yet, to a certain extent, we have exactly this in the form of who we are right now: our currently present selves, which are the result of our past selves' decisions, some of which led to positive and some to negative outcomes. We can see what the various decisions we made have led to—obviously, combined with a whole bunch of external influences; but to a large extent, with fortitude, we could all be in a better present predicament were it not for our less than optimal past selves' decisions.

In a way, the solution to our problem (the cure to the disease) is to improve our skills in what is now called "mental time travel," namely, how well and how far we can imagine our own futures. This involves a kind of rehearsal or trial run of the future or of possible futures.[11] Indeed, studies related to the fMRI results mentioned above seem to show that how "vividly" one can see one's future self (i.e., how well one can travel ahead in this way) is an extremely strong predictor of delinquency (and, by extension, of flourishing).[12] More evidence for Parfit's basic thesis that connectedness is important, but equally, I would say, evidence that there is hope for interventions that *battle against* the problem by strengthening connections rather than simply accepting that it weakens as time delays are increased. The previous study in fact did exactly this, showing people electronically generated versions of their future selves in order to latch more closely onto them and develop a bond with them. In general, we need to use that region of the brain responsible for thinking about ourselves (self-regions) for thinking about our future selves (if we must speak in this divisive way), rather than the latter residing in our "stranger-regions." One way of establishing this is through a conceptual reorientation: by viewing our present self as simply the future self of our past self, we can project our present self onto the future self more readily. That is, our present self *just is* the future self of our past self! Treat every future time as equally as Now, because it will be Now *later*, and it will be *your* Now—it's so easy to get tangled in tenses here! The idea can be encapsulated in the following simple diagram (fig. 4.1).

Let us change tack a little, to a related but inverse aspect of this disease of time. There's a lot to be said for delaying gratification for the benefit of our future incarnation, for leaving that

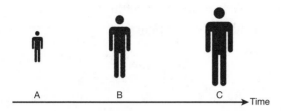

FIGURE 4.1. B is a future self of A, but will be a past self of C. What B does now, will determine C's past. But of course, C's past is what has created him, so B's actions now determine both C and C's past. Likewise, B has A to thank for how he is now: B is a future self of A, and A's actions determined B's past.

marshmallow for later, as the late Walter Mischel encapsulates it. Mischel's *Marshmallow Test*[13] reveals differing strategies among children depending on their environment/background and is a strong predictor of future delinquency and success. The setup is simple: offer children one marshmallow now or the chance to get two if they wait a while. It is interpreted as a self-control issue, but, as Mischel noticed, it is perfectly rational for children in more unstable social conditions to take the marshmallow while they can. Mischel was almost one hundred when he died. He worked until the end, and I had the pleasure of inviting him to a conference on issues covered in this book in 2015. I was most impressed by his incredible, highly original artwork that he made using hospital x-ray sheets, something he took up in his last years.

So, indeed, prudence can be a fine thing. We have seen how many extremely severe problems have this simple yet pernicious temporal factor (inability to delay gratification) at their root. But, going back to Seneca, one should not go take this to extremes. One should not live *too much* into the future, for that is not actually living. It's a fine art getting the balance right. Indeed, our old friend Seneca was right on the money with this one:

> One hears a lot of people saying, "I'll ease off and take things easy when I'm fifty, and my sixtieth year will release me from duties." And what guarantee of a longer life have you gotten? Who will permit those things to proceed as you've planned them? Aren't you ashamed to set aside the remnants of life for yourself and to devote to higher thought only that portion of time that can't be put to any business matter? How late to begin to live, at the point that life must be left behind! How foolish it is to ignore mortality and put off sound pursuits to one's fiftieth or sixtieth year, and to want to start life at a point to which few have attained![14]

I readily admit to having had this inverted problem from a fairly young age: I will (or would: I'm much better these days) often sacrifice my poor present and near-future self for very-far-in-the-future betterment. Since my very early teenage years, I called this "future-selving" (to which we return in the next chapter). The (now completely obvious) idea that I could spare my future self trouble and make the future better by acting a specific way was an absolute epiphany for me that served me well in some ways, but very badly in others, since I engaged in the practice to a punishing degree from which I'm still recovering (itself the subject of chapter 7).

If I might be allowed to interject an embarrassing confession here: at the time of this epiphany, around the age of twelve, I became thoroughly obsessed with the piano and managed to become very good, very quickly, practicing until my finger-tips split open at the seams of my fingerprints, trying to carve out the future I wanted from the sea of possibilities. I wanted to play a particular, virtuosic piece of music I'd seen on BBC TV's *Young Musician of the Year* competition: Mili Balakirev's *Islamey* (the score of which I bought before I could actually read music and which I memorized and played within two years). Later, when I switched from a music to a philosophy degree, I would put a chair on my mattress and read nonstop for several days without sleep (with a five-day record, at which point I was having hallucinations and waking dreams bordering on schizophrenia), rocking the chair to keep myself awake, in a room peppered wth notes telling myself to "work more now!" I kept a constant focus on making the future as I wanted it (which was to be a *thinker* for my living and somehow solve the problem of why there is something rather than nothing: modest goals . . .), and also to spare my future self as much distress as possible. Pretty bloody pathological, and utterly shocking, bizarre behavior to me in retrospect.

Though in some ways it worked out, I would not recommend this level of future-selving: it does to the present self what we are trying to avoid doing to the future self. Unlike Seinfeld, my present self feels bad for my past self (and no doubt my future self will too): he went rather overboard, that guy! As Jolande Jacobi (one of Carl Jung's students) puts it, "[T]he first half of . . . life was actually lived under the sign of the second."[15] Youth is expended on tasks meant for later—a byproduct of this can be a reversal of the sign of the second half of life into the first, heralding the very real "midlife crisis" marking the turning point.[16]

The 1949 song "Enjoy Yourself (It's Later Than You Think)" (by Carl Sigman and Herb Magidson)[17] puts the problem better than any other example I know in the philosophical literature, even giving Seneca a run for his money:

> You work and work for years and years, you're always on
>   the go
> You never take a minute off, too busy makin' dough
> Someday, you say, you'll have your fun, when you're a
>   millionaire
> Imagine all the fun you'll have in your old rockin' chair
>
> *Chorus:*
> Enjoy yourself, it's later than you think
> Enjoy yourself, while you're still in the pink
> The years go by, as quickly as a wink
> Enjoy yourself, enjoy yourself, it's later than you think
>
> You're gonna take that ocean trip, no matter, come what
>   may
> You've got your reservations made, but you just can't get
>   away
> Next year for sure, you'll see the world, you'll really get
>   around
> But how far can you travel when you're six feet
>   underground?

There can certainly, then, be *overidentifying* with future selves or (say in the case of severe trauma and flashbacks) with past selves. However, I think Seneca oversells this point—though as mentioned in chapter 1, he had good reasons for this. As already mentioned, life was a lot shorter and more volatile in his day, so we need to factor in these golden years, which also are healthier than in Seneca's day. As we will find over and over, life must be a rather skillful balancing act between a pair of poles drawn from Jungian depth psychology: the sagacious *Senex* (the old man: rational, reserved, analytical, and anxious) and the imprudent *Puer* (the eternal child: unruly, irrational, unbounded, and present-focused). Curiously, despite his name, Seneca himself is quite clearly more on the side of the *Puer*, with its carpe diem character—though this carpe diem lifestyle must come only *after* one has done the Senexian hard work in one's youth, thus flipping around what appears to be a more natural pairing of the *Puer* character with the young and the *Senex* character with the old.

Hence, there are two prongs to this particular disease of time, both very bad when taken to extremes: overpresentness (associated with a *Puer* personality type) and overfutureness (associated with a *Senex* type). Both involve *preoccupation* with some aspect of time at the expense of others. Ideally we want to have both poles integrated, to produce a well-rounded, balanced individual: not preoccupied with any times over others. If anything, we should aim for a limbering up to midlife transition. Many a divorce would be avoided. Indeed, the midlife crisis is simply another disease of time from within the same category we have been discussing, in this case caused in part by the awareness of the finite boundary to the future (i.e., death), and the thought that one's "best years" are behind them. Given this realization, any "unlived life" seeks to make itself known before it's too late. People find themselves suddenly in strong agreement with Sigman and Magidson's lyrics.

We face some difficulty here, since our theory of time impacts quite heavily on the way we behave, and there are many such theories. Most people have an implicit theory of time that they could possibly unpack if you asked them to, but they will be nonetheless subliminally guided by it in their actions. If one believes the future is "already real"—as in the block universe picture (in which all events, past, present, and future, exist in a four-dimensional block, the universe, which doesn't change and just *is*), so popular today among physicists and philosophers, which I think is a terrible mistake—then one might feel more powerless in acting *for* some future self. After all, it's a done deal, and one's journey to that self is like Parfit's glass tunnel. It's already happened, a fait accompli.

If one believes, on the other hand, that the future is not yet real, that possibility is a real feature of the universe, then one faces the problem that *anything* might happen, and that beyond very short times, unless one is the biggest control freak in the universe, one will struggle to act for that future self anyway, so that one's "future sculpting" might be interrupted in various unforeseen ways. In the next chapter, we pursue this idea of *sculpting a future* further, linking it to the Jungian concept of *individuation*, which is the process of becoming psychologically whole (in the sense of understanding the drivers of one's actions). It is, after all, no good doing things for your future self if you don't know what is propelling your actions in the first place.

5

Project Me

Every moment I shape my destiny with a chisel. I am a carpenter of my own soul.

—JALAL AD-DIN MUHAMMAD RUMI, *RUMI: IN THE ARMS OF THE BELOVED*[1]

Man is nothing other than his own project.

—JEAN-PAUL SARTRE, *EXISTENTIALISM IS A HUMANISM*[2]

"PROJECT ME" MIGHT suggest utter narcissism on the surface, but here nothing could be further from the truth. I have in mind taking radical responsibility for one's life and poking around in your psyche enough to see what factors are responsible for your actions. There is double meaning to "Project Me": (1) making your future a creative endeavor, and (2) acknowledging your own unconscious projections onto the world and other people, including yourself through the projection of a false self: work out what you are projecting—otherwise you face not the world, but your internal *image* of the world (and the people in it) weighed down by your own internal baggage. Hence, this chapter concerns both *responsibility* for your future and *authenticity* in bringing about a future that is well-aligned to your character.

In the previous chapter, I mentioned an epiphany when I was around twelve years old that utterly transformed my life. Quite simply: I can do things *right now* that will save future me (if we want to use this way of speaking) a lot of trouble, work, or stress. All those times when I regretted *not* doing something annoying or difficult would never again arise if only I did the appropriate actions. One can eliminate regret. Why *wouldn't* I do such a thing, then? And I usually did. And my future self was indeed very thankful, and would sometimes thank past me out loud—I still sometimes do this.

Many readers, probably all, will find this about the most unimpressive epiphany imaginable: a trivial fact of life. But, we have already seen that whether we know our impact on our future or not, we don't always obey and act in our best interests. Neither, I believe, do many people who would agree with the statement (that we can work for our futures by performing the right actions NOW) appreciate the deeper ramifications of that idea.

The future's plasticity is key. We can do much to mold it with action. Often, people stop at the *thought* of action and expect the world to jump into line. This is magical thinking, and of course it has no effect whatsoever on the world out there, beyond a few neurons jiggling in a slightly different way as a result of the thought. Acts of will involve putting the world into motion. This is the pruning process mentioned in the preface: by acts of will (decisions made in the face of choices), one selects a way the universe *will be* and thereby eliminates ways the universe *could* have been, like so many discarded branches, like so many fragments of marble chiseled away. One simply must adopt this viewpoint for the approach to make sense; otherwise the pernicious disease of temporal discounting threatens to ruin things.

The basic idea is then to treat your life as your own creation, as a kind of malleable sculpture (an opus, or a topiary project if the pruning metaphor works better for you) that you must carve away at right now in the correct way to get the results you desire—it can easily degenerate into the creation of a narcissistic false self, so one must carve with deep deliberation rather than impulsively. You can sculpt how you want to be simply by applying the right procedures.[3] Want to be an amazing musician and think this is what you're supposed to be? Then sacrifice time now. The obstacle standing in the way of not doing so is precisely in viewing as a different person that future musician enjoying all your hard work and sacrifice. Why should they benefit from your misery? They do nothing for you toiling away back here, practicing scales hour after hour.

This is, again, the competitive, multiple-selves view promoted by Derek Parfit. Much as I admire Parfit, I think his view has a lot to answer for. To see this, simply apply the idea from the previous chapter: consider your present self as it is now. Does this feel like a stranger from your relatively recent past? Or do you feel like you have endured, that it is still you? That you are as you are because of the things *you* did back then? That if you had done things differently back then, you now would be different as a result? You will feel that same way in the future: as simply the same entity, only with a larger past.[4] Indeed, we should not even view it as a *sacrifice* at all. Nothing is being sacrificed other than certain possibilities through the choices we make (and, at most, along with them, *possible* future selves). Sacrifice involves giving something up for something else, but in this case we ought not to speak of sacrificing current for future selves. Rather, we are distributing across a single self in such a way to make a better life overall. This involves recognizing the role we play in creating the consciously experienced present moments we always find ourselves occupying: the actions we perform now, in this moment, will partially determine what future present moments contain—if we are rational, we will surely want there to be an upward trajectory in the quality of these.[5] The very notion of applying the concept of sacrifice, ditto altruism, here is seen to be tied to the multiple-selves model and competition. The idea that one is being altruistic to oneself is a categorical mistake responsible for many problems: it is simply not coherent to apply the concepts of altruism and sacrifice to the concept of a single self for the same reason that "Darwin's theory of evolution by natural selection is turquoise" does not express a coherent statement.

It is common to believe, in the light of modern physics (specifically, Einstein's theories of special and general relativity), that the universe does not distinguish events into past, present, and future as we ourselves do: such distinctions are a mental projection brought about by the way we are embedded in a spatiotemporal block that contains all things that have happened, are happening, and will happen. But our way of cutting up this four-dimensional world is just a "stubbornly persistent illusion," as Einstein once expressed it.[6] But I think this is a dangerous view, and in fact a kind of natural counter-part to Parfit's multiple-selves view of identity over time, which compels us to view the selves over time as standing in various pregiven relationships to one another, no different in status from spatial relations to other people. And, indeed, Parfit's view also calls on us to treat separation from other people (and their needs) as no different from separation of our future selves in time to such an extent that it can become *selfish* to privilege the temporal relation over the spatial relation. Amusingly, this dissolution of the self (of personal identity over time), as not so fundamental, has been linked to Buddhism, with an affinity so strong that Harvard professor of ethics and public health Dan Wikler was able to get a monastery of Tibetan monks to add passages from Parfit's book *Reasons and Persons* to their chanting practice.[7]

I used to be a fully paid-up member of this so-called block universe view (a "blockhead," to employ philosopher John Earman's phrase[8]) in which all events are laid out in an unchanging four-dimensional array—folly of one's youth, don't you know. I now favor a view more closely associated with William James, who, coincidentally, was the first person to use the expression "block universe"—as a term of disparagement. He was against such a position precisely because it left no door open for possibilities and their elimination (and selection) through acts of will, in other words: for carving. There is no "loose play" in a "blockworld," as James puts it. Instead: "necessity on the one hand and impossibility on the other are the sole categories of the real."[9] James thought that the notion of a *Universe* was itself too rigid a concept, because it suggests a single block. He preferred to think in terms of a "Pluriverse," a world constantly under construction that comes into being in dribs and drabs and, sometimes, with conscious intervention.

On James's view, known as pragmatism, when there is no piece of evidence that could distinguish between a pair of opposing philosophical viewpoints (so that they are *merely* metaphysical), then one should choose the one that makes life go best.[10] We can't really tell whether the world is a block without possibility or something being carved as we go, so we have a choice. A blockworld is as it sounds: rigid, immovable, unmalleable, fixed, eternal, and other such synonyms. It can't change because it contains all times within its structure, so there is nothing external against which it can evolve. This does not fit so well with the idea that we should view our future as a sculpture to be refined. In a four-dimensional block, there are no branches to prune, no excess marble to chisel away at.

Let us turn to a slightly different (though related) element of this project of self-creation, which involves the aforementioned genuine sacrifices. Very often, we know very well what is good for us, but rather than temporal discounting alone, there is a real fear over *making decisions*. If one is free to choose, then one is also responsible for the consequences. Given the one-way nature of time, such consequences can be irreversible: here is a sacrifice. I consider this the greatest of all sacrifices, for one is eradicating ways the universe could be (including the eradication of ways you could be). This is the source of the fear (and I think it is a well-motivated fear: those who do not fear it simply don't understand it), but at the same time the source of meaning, and so vital to the creative enterprise I am discussing. Sartre famously included this kind of inaction in his concept of *mauvaise foi*, or bad faith. We are, as he put it, "condemned to be free."[11] By sticking with the safe, easy, default "choice" and failing to recognize the multitude of other options that are available, a person places himself at the whims of the world. Such a person is more akin to an object than to a conscious human being, or, in Sartrean terms, more akin to a "being-in-itself" than a "being-for-itself." Many people feel helpless against the future. They don't feel they have control over what it might bring, allowing it to happen to them rather than them happening to it. They indeed live much like the quip of Groucho Marx (often the more insightful Marx, in my view . . .), that "life is a whim of several billion cells to be you for a while."[12] But it is not a whim, or at least it needn't be: *you* dictate what these cells do and where they go. You dictate whether they lie on the sofa or get outside and exercise, not the outer universe—the final chapter will consider just how remarkable this feature of reality (that you have a role in how it goes) is. In one way, it is the most obvious and mundane feature of reality, but considered more closely, it is the most miraculous feature of reality.

However, so far we have only considered the very shallowest aspects of Project Me. Individuation in its truest form says that consciousness is overrated, or at least we need to make sure it is expanded enough to know that it is what is driving us, rather than whatever lies lurking in the cellar. While there is a "natural" form of individuation that helps us grow and provides a certain expansion of consciousness (simply through being a human being), there is an active form too: an unnatural one. The question, to repeat, is, do you want to be passive and let the world happen to you, or do you want to be active and let you happen to the world? Since you know that you do have the power to change things, not to do so is just another example of Sartre's bad faith. Indeed, it would be a case, as Sartre suggests, of behaving as an object rather than a subject. Objects have things done to them. Even being conscious of what is happening is not quite sufficient: subjectivity too can be passive. Rather, it is *agency* that matters, the setting of things into motion in the world. To see this, it is enough to consider how often we do something, and are perfectly conscious of that thing, and yet do not want to do it. We act against ourselves.

This is what individuation, developed by Carl Jung, is about: getting beneath consciousness, since consciousness is still too shallow. If consciousness alone were in charge, then we would not be engaging in these self-destructive behaviors: it is something beyond consciousness. This is the way of depth psychology, of course. It is to take control of the process of growth, to take control of the thoughts one believes are the product of one's conscious self and subject them to analysis. To go ever deeper into the psyche. How can we create a future if we do not study the processes driving our beliefs in what we wish to create? We need to be in charge of the decisions. Sometimes when we feel most strongly about something, that is the time to be suspicious!

Jung is not popular among contemporary philosophers, and not all that popular among contemporary psychologists. He's seen as rather old-fashioned, with bizarre views about a hidden, collective order guiding human action and thought (the "collective unconscious"), as well as a belief in strange moments in the universe where the outer world matches your inner world in a meaningful way as if the world were speaking to your emotional needs ("synchronicity"), driven by this hidden order. I think it is a great shame to discredit him, and I think his views, while quaint as expressed in his day, are not so bonkers as is often made out. Indeed, I think his ideas about individuation (and the shadow, on which more later) are among the most important ideas ever discovered by humankind. We ignore them at our peril.

Jung himself was a cheeky sort, always with a pipe to hand and a sly grin. He was no saint either, but this is precisely to be expected given his views, as I will describe in a moment. In his own later memoirs and reflections on life, the universe, and everything, he wrote, "The meaning of my existence is that life has addressed a question to me."[13] In brief: "I myself am a question." As he explained, it is his job to answer that question lest it be answered by the world instead. This is exactly the approach to life I am promoting. It is about extracting a personality out from beneath a whole bunch of complexes, fears, and unconscious drivers of our actions, and then building in accordance with this. Indeed, within philosophy, "the problem of individuation" refers to the problem of figuring out in virtue of what some object is what it is. It is the mark of distinction of some thing. For Jung, it is a dredging process: bringing unconscious elements into the open air, to become whole. If one does not do this, then there is always the possibility of some lurking neurosis sabotaging one's life, controlling the action offstage. One is living, if anything, someone else's life.

Of course, there are real barriers to individuation. There are patterns (the very things one is seeking to unearth) that obstruct the process. Some people are simply not concerned with such things, protected by a veil of ignorance. Others desperately want to feel whole, but they find their ways boobytrapped by various things, often past trauma replaying, especially attachment problems. If one did not grow up with a safe base, then one struggles to find ways of leaving whatever base has been created in the aftermath.[14] Individuation is a process of leaving whatever safe zone you might think you have constructed for yourself, mitigating all risks. It can lead to quite significant disassembly of the self if one has enough defenses operating—at the extreme end, some have *become* their package of defenses, overlapping with a false creation presented to the world to protect them from it (we turn to this issue in chapter 7).

Individuation in Jung's sense is the act of will involved in unearthing the various mechanisms at work. This involves a whole bunch of new ways of observing—dreams, active imagination, and other symbolic work[15]—functioning much like the physicist's development of particle accelerators to reveal the inner structure of atoms. Just as most people can get around the world without understanding the inner structure of atoms (after all, we don't appear to encounter such stuff directly), in the same way most people get around without understanding the inner structure of their selves. But this is much like going on Seneca's nonjourney, simply being "tossed around." Understanding a life is paramount in living it well, for otherwise one has no idea why it went the way it did, and one will have no active way to steer it, like a rock on which waves are crashing, knowing not why or when the next wave will come. What will one have at the end? Merely a series of happenings. Schopenhauer put the importance of this conscious approach nicely in the following metaphor (and indeed, he was a source of inspiration for Jung):

The first forty years of life furnish the text, while the remaining thirty supply the commentary; without the commentary we are unable to understand aright the true sense and coherence of the text, together with the moral it contains.[16]

One of the nice things about this idea is that a tough life makes for a better read later on. It is common to partition life into various stages (or ages) like this. We have already briefly mentioned the clash between *Puer* and *Senex*. However, we might find ways to subdivide this into a finer structure. The Romans further divided into *Juvenis* and *Vir*, lying between these two poles, each with their own associated temporal stances. Of course, Jaques in Shakespeare's *As You Like It* separated out seven ages of Man, entering as an infant "Mewling and puking in the nurse's arms" and ending, in the last scene, with a "second childishness and mere oblivion, sans teeth, sans eyes, sans taste, sans everything."[17] Not such a pretty prospect.

The goal of individuation is, then, to *become whole*, to generate an overlap of what was unconscious with what is conscious. In the next chapter, we see an example of a complex (*puer aeternis*) in which this inner and outer rift causes problems. The problem, we will see, has precisely to do with acting in what appears to be a "follow your inner voice" kind of way, but which is really unanalyzed and unconscious. This goes back to the pruning of possibilities mentioned above: if you are making decisions so powerful as to eliminate entire futures from the universe, then you had better know what forces are guiding this process! You should know if it is really *you* calling the shots, or some archaic injury. We have reason to be fearful of viewing things this way, and individuation is the best prophylactic. Ultimately, it is nothing but paying attention to your thoughts, actions, and beliefs.

<Begin Rant> One wonders why schools don't introduce some program to teach psychology (including the idea of individuation) to children. After all, we are humans, and need to know how they (and how *we ourselves*) work, as much as we need to know about bunsen burners and BOD-MAS. The assumption is, I suppose, that simply by being around other children they will learn by some kind of immersion how people work. This is absolute nonsense, and the common crises that emerge in midlife attest to this. We might know about the external behaviors of others, but nowhere is one taught how to understand one's inner life and experience. If done early, this could help avoid a whole bunch of neuroses, traumas, attachment issues, divorces, and broken families downstream. Prepare children for their futures in a *realer* sense than simply being work-ready. Surely this ought to be the *most* compulsory of lessons: life! <End Rant>

Meanwhile, if like me (and unlike Parfit and the Buddhists) you view death as important, then you might go to the following webpage to stimulate the process of individuation and get started on your own Project Me journey: www.mainfacts.com /time-life-countdown-timer. To figure out your (best-case scenario for) remaining life by seeing it in the number of days left is somewhat distressing. I see that even if I live to the ripe old age of one hundred, I have only 20,563 days left to live. That sounds like very few to me, regardless of Seneca's remarks to the contrary. But unless one is living authentically and with purpose, one is not really living at all. In this case, consider the countdown to be rather the number of days remaining to create a real life you can be proud of, rather than a death timer.

6

The Provisional Life

BORIS: *Something's missing.*
DOCTOR: *What?*
BORIS: *I don't know, I feel a void at the center of my being.*
DOCTOR: *What kind of void?*
BORIS: *Well . . . an empty void.*
DOCTOR: *An empty void?*
BORIS: *Yes. I felt a full void about a month ago but it was just something I ate.*

—WOODY ALLEN, *LOVE AND DEATH*[1]

There's always a hair in the soup.

—MARIE-LOUISE VON FRANZ,
THE PROBLEM OF THE PUER AETERNUS[2]

HELTON GODWIN BAYNES (1882–1943) was an English supporter of C. J. Jung's psychoanalytic views, translating some of his works, as well as writing his own rather fine books. He is perhaps best-known for his elucidation of Jung's phrase "the provisional life."[3] Baynes characterized this phenomenon as "a state of childish irresponsibility and dependence" manifesting as ennui. It points to a stunted psychological development, stuck in adolescence, still dependent on a mother. It is life without life, Seneca's "long tossing about" in place of "a long voyage" (as mentioned in the first chapter).

If you view your current life circumstances, your projects, your relationships as mere placeholders, waiting for things to change or wanting to do something different but never actually doing so, then you are living the provisional life. Always looking elsewhere, to the future, to other people, to other ways of being, and never settling and committing to what you have, or else putting in the time and energy to actively achieve what you want. We might call this "onedayism": one day I'll get around to making a decision once and for all. Seneca, in his *Moral Epistles* to Lucilius (in a letter titled "On Saving Time"), writes, "[E]mbrace every hour since the result will be that you'll depend less on tomorrow, if you're taking today in your hands. As we delay, life is rushing past."[4]

The provisional life is an inauthentic life in the sense that some inner picture is not being realized in the world. However, most often there is no clear picture in the first place, only a hazy feeling of general discontent that things are not as they ought to be: an empty void . . .

Jung's most famous student, Marie-Louise von Franz, describes the phenomenon as the feeling that

one is not yet in real life. For the time being one is doing this or that thing, but whether it is a woman or a job, it is not yet what is really wanted, and there is always the fantasy that

sometime in the future the real thing will come about. . . .
The one thing dreaded throughout by such a typical man is
to be bound to anything whatever. There is a terrific fear of
being pinned down, of entering space and time completely,
and of being the specific human being that one is. There is
always the fear of being caught in a situation from which it
may be impossible to slip out again. Every just-so situation
is hell.[5]

She goes on: "The woman also is never quite the right woman;
she is nice as a girlfriend, but - . There is always a 'but' which
prevents marriage or any kind of definite commitment."[6] Now,
I'm going to be brutally honest here, and lay my neck on the
chopping block: Confession No. 2. In writing this book, I am
simultaneously attempting to write away a *Puer*-dominance
in myself, which probably emerged precisely as a reaction to
having lived as an old man too early (now ludicrously doing
here what you're supposed not to do: dealing with it ratio-
nally, through writing!). This is terribly un-English of me, so
cover your eyes and jump the paragraph if this is simply too
unseemly . . .

Following a rather messy separation and no small measure of
Don Juanism (see below), I found a truly exceptional woman.
Despite several years together, I struggled to bring myself to
"seal the deal" ("one day . . ."—I expect this book to help *me*
too in this respect). This is exactly the kind of blockage that
von Franz refers to. It is fear-based and the fear centers exactly
on the issue of the irreversibility of certain decisions, on sacrificing possibilities: on being bounded. On committing. It is
avoidant. Yet, as Jung puts it, "[T]he meaning of life is surely

that it is lived, not avoided."[7] We want the real thing. We want to be sure. And in this attitude we end up bringing about provisionality, which we don't want. The anxiety then arises precisely as a result of finitude, of the shortness of life. Our space of possibilities is ever-shrinking as we age, and we want to retain as many branches as possible to avoid irreversible choices that prune these, taking precious life along with them. There are, quite simply, fewer branches to prune as we march through life.

The standard view is that such "puerism" is linked to a mother complex. It is a search for the perfect mother: "a woman who will bring perfect love, perfect warmth, perfect harmony, a lasting relationship." Such perfection does not exist, of course, so *Puers* bounce from one thing to the next as soon as imperfections are noticed. Fantasies take over because they can at least give some semblance of perfection, being unreal (surely unreality is the worst of imperfections, but this *is* a neurosis here!).

Following standard psychoanalytic procedure, Jung associated this neurosis with a character from Greek mythology: Bacchus (or Dionysus). Ovid, writing of the Eleusinian mysteries in his *Metamorphoses* (also the source of the "narcissism" terminology, and there are in fact strong links between these two pathological personality types, especially as regards grandiosity), described Bacchus as an eternal youth (*puer aeternus*). Youth is, of course, defined by its absence of responsibility. The Bacchus complex does not seem to have stuck however, and the *puer aeternus* label seems to be standard. Von Franz prefers to couch her discussion in terms of Antoine de Saint-Exupéry's *The Little Prince*.[8]

Jung himself believed that work is the only fix for pathological irresponsibility, involving a step toward the opposite pole or shadow archetype.[9] Here is von Franz again, speaking about her mentor's viewpoint:

> I remember him saying to a *puer aeternus* type, "It does not matter what job you take. The point is that for once you do something thoroughly and conscientiously, whatever it is." This man insisted that if only he could find the right occupation, then he would work, but that he could not find it. Dr. Jung's answer was, "Never mind, just take the next bit of earth you can find. Plough it and plant something in it. No matter whether it is business, or teaching, or anything else, give yourself for once to that field which is ahead of you." Everybody has in front of him a field of reality where he can work if he wants to, and the childish trick of saying, "I would work if it were the right thing," is one of the many self-delusions of the *puer aeternus*, by which he keeps within the mother and his megalomanic identification with the god—because the gods, as you know, do not work.[10]

We might think he should be only referring to *meaningful* work. Without this, any budding Bacchus will feel like that other mythical figure, Sisyphus, punished by eternally pushing a rock up a hill after it rolls down from one side to the other. Here we go back to a key theme from the preface: limitation. The *Puer* feels like a god, as Jung rightly says: immortal, eschewing limits. Work is certainly limiting, and that is the point of Jung's suggesting *any* work, fit for gods or otherwise. Albert Camus famously compared the human condition to this myth (in his 1942 work *The Myth of Sisyphus*).[11] It seems like a life with no point. A struggle with no ultimate goal in sight. Camus's solution to some extent matches Jung's own: accept the struggle, accept even the absurdity of one's situation, and don't worry so much about looking elsewhere for happiness.

What Jung wanted from his work solution really was the act of being fully involved in something. Of giving in to something. Something *real*. Of committing. Fully encapsulated in the space and time one inhabits, rather than merely prodding at the horizon thinking about what one could be doing and how much better it would be than this.[12] It demands a radical acceptance of one's non-Godlike nature. It is deflation in its best, most productive, and quickest form. It is, moreover, what *adults* do!

Perhaps this can explain something of the *Puer*'s listlessness: without an acceptance of the stages of aging, of the natural limits that come with each stage, they fail to access the meaning that death provides, and so they are bored and looking for the next big thing. The *Puer* readily agrees with the *I Ching* that unlimited possibilities are not suited to humans: but they are not ordinary humans; they are special! That is the drawback of getting in touch with reality (though this is exactly what is required to avoid complications), because in that way one becomes limited: there are restrictions. One comes instead to the miserable, absurd, human situation where one's hands are tied and it is not possible to do as one would like, something that is particularly disagreeable to the *puer aeternus*. What one produces is always miserable compared to the fantasies one had lying in bed dreaming about what one would do if one could just get around to it, or if people recognized one's talents! How can the real world ever come close to a fantasy? But neither should we so readily underestimate the *Puer*'s reluctance to

commit to important life events, nor put it down to some irrationality (at least, not in all cases). It is possible that they simply
understand the magnitude of commitment all too well, and in
fact take it more seriously than those who causally jump head-
first into the deep end. Decisions are as much a destructive act
as a creative one, killing off alternatives to allow a single one
to live.

Philosophers have long battled with the distinction between
appearance and reality. Plato, perhaps most famously, introduced the notion of ideal Forms of which reality could only
provide highly imperfect copies. Indeed, there was a whole
story coming from Plato's theory (as described in his *Timaeus*)
related to Gnostic ideas in which a demiurge (a divine craftsman) attempts to build a world of material things that matched
the realm of the ideal forms as closely as possible. The Gnostic
tradition took up this story and turned the demiurge into a vil-
lain (the Old Testament god) who created the evil universe we
inhabit, thereby separating us from the ideal, spiritual world to
which we truly belong.

Many people live their lives with some ideal image in mind,
especially when it comes to their love lives, as if this is something that they ought to strive for, like the Gnostics feeling like
the material world is not enough. Marcel Proust put it best in
the third book from his masterpiece, *In Search of Lost Time: The
Guermantes Way*:

> It is the wicked deception of love that it begins by making us
> dwell not upon a woman in the outside world but upon a doll
> inside our head, the only woman who is always available in
> fact, the only one we shall ever possess, whom the arbitrary

nature of memory, almost as absolute as that of the imagination, may have made as different from the real woman as the real Balbec had been from the Balbec I imagined—a dummy creation that little by little, to our own detriment, we shall force the real woman to resemble.[13]

To a certain extent, *everything* begins as a kind of doll inside our head. We project our entire world in the sense that this world exists partially as a process in our brains. The trick to authenticity is to try and make inner and outer match as faithfully as possible. To take back one's projections and see the world as it is, or else make it as one would desire it to be through action.

Interestingly, Camus mentions the legend of Don Juan in his book *The Myth of Sisyphus*, as a way of escaping the absurdity of life by effectively embracing the lack of rules or fixed order. Albert Camus connected Don Juanism to what is essentially puerism in his discussion of what he calls "The Absurd Man."[14] An absurd man is one who is consistent with existentialism: it involves an understanding (even if only noncognitively) that life is ultimately meaningless. Camus points out that the Don Juan does not seek any kind of meaningful life whatsoever.

This is, of course, an old and well-loved legend, inspiring not least Mozart's opera *Don Giovanni* and Lord Byron's epic poem, *Don Juan*. The full title of Mozart's opera is *Il dissoluto punito, ossia il Don Giovanni*, which refers to "The Libertine [or rake[15]] Punished." Of course, the legend is most strongly associated with sexual escapades, and indeed the label "Don Juan" now refers to a rather superficial school of "pickup artistry" in which the aim is to seduce as many women as possible by using all kinds of tricks and treating the entire enterprise as a game. But, probing more deeply, Don Juan's sexual escapades are laced with a rather "puerish" purpose in mind: he is seeking an ideal woman. In other words: a dummy creation.

Given this depth to the legend, it is not surprising that the Don Juan personality comes in for the psychoanalytic treatment. Perhaps the most famous serious study is that of Otto Rank, in his book *The Don Juan Legend*.[16] Otto Rank, a student of Freud (excommunicated, like Jung, for having the temerity to disagree with the great man), was both the lover and the psychotherapist of diarist and novelist Anaïs Nïn, certainly a *puella aeternus* (or Dona Juana) in her own right. Rank's work on creativity in women triggered Nïn's grandiosity, so he was added to her large collection of men (which also included Henry Miller, Gore Vidal, and, if we are to believe her diaries, even her own father) while she lived parasitically on her husband, Hugh Guiler (a codependent if ever there was one). Curiously, she did commit to one man, Rupert Pole, later in her life, as well as seemingly accepting her finitude (albeit as a result of an aggressive cervical cancer), and ended her days in a more meaningful condition.[17]

Rank's discussion centers on exactly the themes we have raised here and on those raised by Camus. Namely, "the relationship between individuals and their own ego and the threat of its complete destruction by death."[18] He introduces the notion of "the double," which is a close cousin of Jung's own notion of "the shadow," and finds expression of this concept in various myths and stories, including the myth of narcissus, Robert Louis Stevenson's *Dr Jekyll and Mr Hyde*, and Oscar Wilde's *Picture of Dorian Gray*. Rank can never quite detach from his old mentor's oedipal interpretations, however. But the correlation between the lack of meaning and the inability to commit (and limit) is clear to see.

For Jung, this *Puer* is one of the clearest examples of the many archetypes that drive us. The *Senex* (wise old man) is its shadow. Living too much under either archetype leads to troubles, but so too does living them at the wrong stages of life. Living a *Puer*-dominant existence in later stages, following a *Senex*-dominant younger life, is a recipe for disaster since the finite boundary cannot fail to make its presence felt, along with resentment at the lost opportunities of youth.

We have seen this already, albeit in different terms, in the previous chapters, in which people can have very differing temporal perspectives that possess their own complementary virtues and vices. It might be useful to illustrate these with a table.[19]

Puer	*Senex*
Immortal (unbounded/infinite)	Mortal (bounded/finite)
Present-oriented (procrastination)	Future-oriented (anxiety)
Irrational	Rational
Irresponsible	Responsible
Invulnerable	Vulnerable
Meaningless	Meaningful

Jung and von Franz appeared to have violated their own principles of "shadow work" (namely, that one must have a little of both of a complementary pair to have a fully integrated, wholesome personality), pretty much dismissing all *Puer* characteristics as bad—indeed, the very title of von Franz's book is called *the problem* of the *puer aeternus*! But like almost all characteristics, the *Puer* has many great qualities that should only be part of a balanced whole. Given the table of qualities, moreover, we see that it is required in order to not be too preoccupied with nonpresent times. Ultimately, as relates to the previous chapter, what matters is that one is conscious and in control of one's life.

James Hillman, another Jungian psychologist (responsible for the approach known as "archetypal psychology"), appeared to go entirely in the opposite direction from Jung and von Franz. Australian analytical psychologist David Tacey[20] speaks of Hillman as waging a "psychological war" against what he saw as selling out to normalcy, instead singing the praises of the *Puer* and scoffing at the idea that we should bring the *Puer* down to earth (what spoilsports!):

> To reduce the fantasies, dry the hysterics, confront the intuitions, bring down to earth and reality, turn the poetry into prose. The will is to direct sexuality into relationship; the crippling is to be overcome through the exercise of work, practicality, sacrifice, limits, hardening. The face is to be set, positions defended, the provisional overcome through the panacea of commitment.[21]

There is that word again: "limits." I have been arguing that limits are the very stuff of meaning. Our actions in the face of choices limit the world by eliminating the options not taken. This combination of limitation via action is at the heart of a meaningful existence. While it might start with an upswing, life becomes a dysfunctional downward spiral without imposing such limits. But this is not to say that I agree with Jung and von Franz's idea that one should essentially "break in" a *Puer*, as if it were some kind of errant racehorse. Here, I think David Tacey has it right when he says, "[T]o advocate the puer as a psychological style would never deliver eternal childhood, merely eternal puerility."[22] The problem, in other words, is that the psychological profile becomes more unsavory and indeed unsustainable with age. But, as Hillman explained, it can go in the other direction too, and so he speaks of "curing the senex problem" with a dash of *Puer* spirit.[23] This should really be obvious from the above table, in which we see either stance, adopted in isolation, is problematic.

Really, there is not the difference Hillman speaks of; he clearly misunderstands that the solution offered by Jung and von Franz is implicitly calling on the very concepts Hillman himself uses: *Senex* and *Puer*. Work and grounding are precisely *Senex*, and elsewhere Jung and von Franz point out that too much *Senex*, after making a commitment (a *Senex* thing to do), can lead to stagnation.[24] Tacey interprets Hillman as so far under the spell of the mother complex that he has no chance to see his own situation from outside and recognize that he is exhibiting precisely the problematic parts of the complex and the *Puer* phenomenon. I agree: Hillman always put the "*puer* problem" in scare quotes: not only did he suffer from the *Puer*-complex, he also suffered from a (*Puer*-complex)-complex!

As with Seneca's views, which like Jung and von Franz also suggest a grounding of sorts (in real rather than provisional living), we must take into account the specific age of his target. While Paulinus had undoubtedly benefited from his earlier drive to succeed in Rome, enlarging his life, at some stage one simply eats into what little remains with pursuits unfit to fill so precious a resource as time. A little "early puering" might not be so bad, perhaps. But, it is true that unless such folks do slow down, they will inevitably burn out. As Billy Joel once expressed in "Vienna," "You're gonna kick off before you even get halfway through."[25] It is a useful exercise to try and identify *Puers* in the entertainment industry that suffered in this way: it is chock full of them, with many (and this word is fully apt) *premature* deaths, certainly way in excess of the number of such in a randomly chosen sample (the so-called 27 Club is a case in point, which boasts among its members the three Js: Janis Joplin, Jim Morrison, and Jimi Hendrix).

Perhaps the clearest and most obvious example of all was Michael Jackson, who lived so much as a Peter Pan, never wanting to grow up, that he even named his home Neverland![26] Of course, we can easily trace his puerism to the theft of his actual childhood by a tyrannical father. In other ways, however, Michael Jackson is not like a *Puer* as characterized by Jung: for he worked to excessive levels with no miraculous cure. Rather, as he worked harder and harder, he simultaneously appeared to be attempting to become younger and younger (with ultimately damaging plastic surgeries). This is most likely due to a mixing of pathologies, in this case with concomitant perfectionism. There are a whole bunch of such related pathologies having to do with former child prodigies that have a similar flavor. To survive the famous "transition," they simply must embrace some *Senex*. There are a great many cases of those who didn't and became neurotic or perished, often as a result of some addiction. Here we can name the great Polish pianist Josef Hofmann, who after a career already spanning several years was rescued at the age of twelve by the Society for the Prevention of Cruelty to Children, who intervened, arranging it so that he could only play in public again at the age of eighteen. But the damage was already done, and he became an alcoholic, progressively damaging his abilities.

The next chapter will go further into the *puer aeternus* complex itself and the havoc it can wreak at its limits.

7

Bulletproofing

Remember the number one rule of biohacking—first remove the things that are making you weak (or old).

—DAVE ASPREY, *SUPER HUMAN*[1]

Dave Asprey is a rather astute businessman who has a goal to become 180 years old. He brought out an entire range of "Bulletproof" health and optimality products for brain and body. The punchline of this chapter is not that bulletproofing is bad per se, but rather that one should bulletproof in the right way. Bulletproofing could easily suggest *avoidance*. One of Jung's students, Jolande Jacobi, expressed it perfectly:

> It is not the length of life and not its freedom from disturbance which are the decisive factors in the success of individuation but, as we have seen, the draining of life to the full, in the good and difficult alike.[2]

This is a very Stoic-like statement, highly reminiscent of Seneca. Jacobi works the stages of life into this viewpoint, however, ultimately agreeing with Seneca that even a short life "which compresses all the phases into a short time, can be brought to full maturity and rounded out, as we can see from numerous outstanding personalities who were already wise in their youth."[3]

A natural tendency for many humans is to try and make themselves impervious to any and all attack: bulletproofing. This comes from an understandable place: a desire not to be hurt. To be invulnerable. But one has to be aware of the costs of taking this too far. Every new piece of armor pushes some piece of the self into the shadow world from which it can invisibly control actions. If one does this enough, the self that remains in view is some kind of powerful, shiny beast that can take anything on. The British psychoanalyst Jean Arundale calls this shiny beast "the fortress of I."[4] This fortress, while protective, renders its inhabitant's universe a solipsistic and lonely one. Really, it is more like a scab that forms to protect a vulnerable interior. The Asprey quote we began this chapter with suggests such an image (e.g., of a perfect body or mind), such that any deviation from the image is dealt with swiftly and harshly.

To a certain extent, there is much to like about the emphasis on actively creating your future self, but there is a slippery slope from this kind of idealization to pathology. For example, it is a short step from body obsession to bulimia or some kind of body dysmorphic disorder. Any deviation, however minor, is perceived as a *flaw* or a weakness. We tend to think of this as a mostly female issue; it can, however, take the form of muscle dysmorphia that afflicts many bodybuilders and can lead them to what are obviously unhealthy practices, such as anabolic steroid use. This can be viewed as a situation in which there is an overvaluing of the future; one damages a present self to attempt to secure some desired future self. Only in this case it is far worse because the image is often unrealistic. This mostly results in a worse life for both selves.

No doubt many social anxieties boil down to generic dysmorphias, in which the reality of oneself can never quite match up to the ideal, and so one cannot possibly expose the world to such a flawed specimen: the horror![5] This relates to the authenticity component of carving your future self, for one has to be very careful that the self created is not some idealized concoction invented partially through a series of past traumas or some complexes, or some ideal image that has been essentially implanted by current social trends.

A significant male form of psychological bulletproofing is precisely the *puer aeternus* complex discussed in the previous chapter. This complex presupposes gender roles and might not be so popular these days. However, I think it has much to teach us. The Jungian analyst and self-acknowledged, quasi-reformed *Puer*, Daryl Sharp, expresses this specific aspect of the complex very nicely, in terms that neatly fit our discussion:

> Puers have various components, the key one of which can be applied to both men and women: an inability to commit. This does not simply refer to relationships, but to any task that becomes in any way onerous. They seek perfection in partners. They seek perfection in life, but not in a way that involves dogged pursuit with delayed gratification.[6]

Puers really do not cope well with delayed gratification: it is a limitation, a commitment of sorts. A commitment to the future. Again, Daryl Sharp perfectly encapsulates the idea:

> Plans for the future slip away in fantasies of what will be, what could be, while no decisive action is taken to change. He covets independence and freedom, chafes at boundaries and limits, and tends to find any restriction intolerable.[7]

As he goes on to point out, there is common imagery of *imprisonment* terrorizing the *Puer*, but the bars are of his own making. From the outside, the solution looks rather simple: break out! Make a choice and live with the consequences, good or bad. Live! But from the inside, such decisions trigger mortal terror. Any shift from comfort whatsoever presents a potentially existential disruption. So better not to do anything at all. Play it safe. Yet the real bars are the way to freedom, as the final chapter will argue. For what is freedom but the enforcing of a decisive act of will? The freedom to act. And what is this decisive action other than foregoing alternatives in favor of one outcome: of committing to it? Of putting oneself behind bars. Yet bulletproofing is inherently avoidant. It anticipates threat.

A more dangerous aspect of puerism (shared by narcissism in the real, *personality disorder* sense) is that it can lead to grandiosity or inflation: boundlessness. This might not sound like a bad thing, but if one believes in a grandiose image of oneself (or others, or even the world), then one will rarely live up to it.[8] This is a more extreme dysmorphia, manifesting in an attack on one's very identity, rather than one's body or some aspect of it. If one believes one should *be* a certain way, a certain kind of self, and one fails to attain that, then clearly there is the risk of genuine annihilation if that ideal is not attained. Such a phenomenon often arises in a relationship setting, especially with Cluster B sufferers,[9] in which it appears as an initial overidealization of the love-object that cannot fail to be shattered and brought down to earth. Parents can also overidealize their children too, generating an unachievable ideal form, resulting in inevitable shame in the child (often resulting in a Cluster B pathology, in fact), in not being able to reach or sustain the perfectionist impulse. Harking back to the examples of prodigies in the previous chapter, a sad example of this can be seen in the case of the Australian pianist Geoffrey Tozer, whose outstanding talents were aggressively pushed by his emotionally incestuous mother. He drunk himself to death after, in his and many others' minds, under-achieving and wasting his gift.

Of course, the original myth of narcissism, as told in Ovid's *Metamorphosis* book 3.337, was a cautionary tale.[10] The self-love was damaging, but not only to Narcissus himself, but to those who loved him. It was Echo who suffered because she could not connect with him. But in the psychological version it is not self-love at all, of course. It is love of a *false* self only: the fortress of I. A construction, made usually as a defensive reaction to trauma, or to support overly high expectations, to shield the real self from further attack or from the withdrawal of approval. The false self is precisely supposed to provide core identity bulletproofing: an emotional missile defense system. The following lines from Ovid's poem are particularly apt in this regard: "[H]e gazes at that false image with unsated eyes, and loses himself in his own vision." The problem is, to continue: "What you perceive is the shadow of reflected form: nothing of you is in it."[11] Perfectionists, in this sense, are like Platonists about their various life aspects (relationships, self, work, etc.). The thing about Platonic Forms is that the real world will never live up to them, always amounting to an impoverished shadow cast onto the cave wall.

Still, you might think, with some justification, that the *Senex* archetype, firmly grounded in reality, is rather boring while the *Puer* is exciting. It's quite true. But we are concerned here with living properly during our short time. *Puers* more than most do not live self-consciously. They are bounced around by their deep complexes. To stop and ask why they act as they do is no fun at all—not when it feels so good! The Jungian psychoanalyst James Hollis refers to (negative) patterns from one's past as "hauntings."[12] We are often troubled by ghosts: experiences that persist. Here a remark by Jung himself is instructive:

> No matter how much parents and grandparents have sinned against the child, the man who is really adult will accept these sins as his own condition which has to be reckoned with. Only a fool is interested in other people's guilt. He will ask himself: Who am I that all this should happen to me?[13]

As with other passages from Jung, there is strong flavor of stoicism here. It once again goes back to the choice to be passive or an active force in the universe, and to carry out that task, one must follow that old maxim ascribed to the Delphic oracle carved into the Temple of Apollo: "Know thyself." Unless one has this self-knowledge, whether one is passive or active in the universe is not established.

Bulletproofing can be seen, then, as a form of classic neuroticism: an inability to accept how one is—or at least to fail to root out any components that might not belong and that are controlling us without our knowledge—and build one's world in accordance with this. Again, being healthy and fit is one thing, but being bulletproof is tantamount to being invulnerable. The flight from vulnerability is then no more than a form of self-flagellation.

In a small way, this fights against the Sartrean inessentialism of chapter 4, for we are saying that there is some core that you are. Something you were meant to be, if only you can make the elements guiding your behaviors manifest. Your essence. Your true self. There are times when one feels this in an almost bodily sense. When one knows one is *doing the right thing*: aligning action with purpose. To bulletproof is to push all of the things one doesn't like about oneself under the rug, into one's shadow, rather than becoming comfortable with one's flaws and who one really is. According to Jung's idea of the *shadow*, all of the discarded bits and pieces, supposedly making one weak, will simply lodge elsewhere in the psyche and cause all kinds of trouble. Often what makes one weak is what makes one human.[14]

Crucial to development, and largely in opposition to the bulletproofing concept, is the courageous advance into new life by killing off old life. This is an immensely vulnerable act. One is not pruning the branches by merely intellectually understanding a decision-tree, and understanding cognitively, as it were, that *if* one branch were chosen, *then* the others would disappear. This is rather like reading about wine or music and expecting that to be a sufficient proxy for experiencing them directly.[15] Taking a path requires action, and it will, in many cases, be sufficient to close off alternatives once and for all—for example, once one is a parent, one cannot "unbecome" one! It is nonavoidant. Such is the justified fear of the *Puer*: real, free action has real, significant consequences.

Individuation is, in this sense, at the heart of the pruning of the branches of possibilities. And it is in this same way at the heart of quite possibly the most miraculous, yet mundane, feature of our world: we have a degree of control over how the universe evolves. We determine its structure, even if only in a very small way.[16] I think most people instinctively realize this, and yet they cower and become small in the face of so great a responsibility. Instead, they transform into mere objects and let nature take its course with them. And indeed nature will take its course with you if you let it, guiding your future with its ineluctable logic. We might view, in this way, such appeals to Eastern traditions as a way of calming anxiety (i.e., through meditation) as the worst-possible approach: an utter escape from decision. A *Puer*'s paradise! In such practices, experience is primary, and the Now is primary, but no imprint is made on reality, on the outer world: one simply is as the world is. This is maximal bulletproofing, for there is no self to harm. This might be a positive experience in many ways (as is getting drunk or high), but it is not a cure for anxiety as it arises in a crisis situation. It is avoidance. The way out is to wield this miracle of freedom. But this comes with a sting in the tail, because, to be a broken record, one has to be careful that one's will really is one's will, so that one is not simply impulsively jumping around apparently courageously, but really just recklessly. This is why the individuation process (of making manifest the hidden drivers of one's actions and beliefs) is so vitally important. As Jacobi puts it,

> The freedom of the will extends only as far as the limits of consciousness; as soon as these limits are overstepped, we cease to discriminate, to be capable of conscious choice and judgment, and are delivered over to the uncontrolled impulses and tendencies of the unconscious.[17]

As we saw earlier, the provisional life (avoiding decision) is no sanctuary. While it appears that one is safe from harm (commitment), one is merely bringing death closer:

> Flight from life does not exempt us from the law of age and death. The neurotic who tries to wriggle out of the necessity of living wins nothing and only burdens himself with a constant foretaste of ageing and dying, which must appear especially cruel on account of the total emptiness and meaninglessness of his life.[18]

Bulletproofing is hiding behind a protective screen. And this is precisely a flight from life. Here is von Franz again, as if in response to this chapter's opening quote:

> If you venture into life, into reality, instead of keeping outside so as to avoid suffering, you will find that the earth and women are like a fertile field on which you can work and that life is also death; that if you give yourself to reality, you will be disillusioned and the end of it will be that you will meet death. If you accept your life, you really, in the deepest sense of the word, accept death, and that is what the puer does not want. He does not want to accept mortality, and that is why

he does not want to go into reality, because the end of it is the realization of his weakness and of his mortality. He identifies with the immortal and does not accept the mortal twin, but by going into life he would assimilate the mortal brother.[19]

Such is the fate of the bulletproofer.[20] Perhaps bulletproofing your body and your physical health to a certain extent can be a good thing. But let's not bulletproof our selves, for this leads to a lonely, meaningless existence.[21]

8

The Meaning of ~~Life~~ Death

People usually consider walking on water or in thin air a miracle.
But I think the real miracle is not to walk either on water or in thin
air, but to walk on earth. Every day we are engaged in a miracle
which we don't even recognize: a blue sky, white clouds, green
leaves, the black, curious eyes of a child—our own two eyes. All is a
miracle.

—THICH NHAT HANH, *THE MIRACLE OF MINDFULNESS*[1]

I'm a highly cynical, skeptical chap by disposition. Even putting aside my words about the inherently avoidant nature of such practices in the previous chapter, the notion of "mindfulness" (and the very word itself) bothers my deeply ingrained York-shireman sensibilities. Yet, when the funny words and New-Age-sounding layers are peeled away, it boils down to a solid fact: most of us really are not *present*.[2] Hardly ever. Failing to see this blatant miracle of existence all around, in every object, which, so far as we know, didn't have to be at all—admittedly, it is hard *not* to take everyday reality for granted. Minds often scattered. Pulled this way and that to other things (in the past and the future, and not rooted in reality): To what must be done tomorrow. To what was said to a friend. To what was *not* said to a loved one, but should have been. To that spot on the nose and whether people might see it. Never at rest. Looking out for judgment and rejection from the imaginary audience that follows them around like a marching band. Minds saccading like eyeballs. Never aware. Never still. Certainly not conscious of the hidden drivers of their actions, and so frequently finding themselves puzzled and frustrated by many such of their actions that so often betray them. *Sleepwalking.*

This isn't genuine life, short or long, real or provisional. To borrow Jung's metaphor, this mode of existence is simply akin to a cork's being bobbed around in a rough sea. As Jolande Jacobi (the Jung protégé we met earlier) puts it, it amounts to the difference between "I do" and "I am conscious of what I do."[3] There is mere consciousness, and then there is being conscious *of being conscious.* Of really taking notice. Only with the ability to step back like this can one appreciate the ordinary miracle all around, and can one be said to truly live an examined life.

As philosopher-novelist David Foster Wallace remarked at a 2005 speech at Kenyon College, genuine freedom "means being conscious and aware enough to choose what you pay attention to and to choose how you construct meaning from experience. Because if you cannot exercise this kind of choice in adult life, you will be totally hosed."[4] He continues,

The only thing that's capital-T True is that you get to decide how you're going to try to see it. You get to consciously decide what has meaning and what doesn't. . . . The trick is keeping the truth up-front in daily consciousness.[5]

Here I am put in mind of Terrence McKenna's idea of "radical freedom," according to which you should take control of your own body, mind, and self.[6] If you ignore for the moment that this was told to McKenna by a talking mushroom (it could happen to anyone . . .), the following statement is a good one: "You must have a plan. If you don't, you will become part of somebody else's plan." Seneca said something remarkably similar:

> All those who are preoccupied are in a wretched state, but wretchedest are those who struggle with preoccupations that are not even their own; they sleep in step with the sleep of another, they walk at another's pace. They're under orders as to their loves and hates, the freest of all things. If they want to know how short their own life is, they should consider how small a part of it is their own.[7]

This was partly the job of individuation, as we saw in chapter 5; but there's another element that comes from this basis, which is, as above, to actually then *see* the world in all its glory, and, crucially, to take account of one's noticing: for without your noticing, it is, to return to an earlier theme, pointless. If anything is a miracle, it is the fact that we are here to provide the world with meaning. This is often said to have been eliminated with advances in science. The universe, and we too, are simply the result of a meaningless accident, so the story goes. The Big Bang didn't know we were coming. The American physicist Steven Weinberg expresses this thought, presenting it as part and parcel of the scientific mindset:

> It is almost irresistible for humans to believe that we have some special relation to the universe, that human life is not just a more-or-less farcical outcome of a chain of accidents reaching back to the first three minutes, but that we were somehow built in from the beginning. . . . It is hard to realize that this all [i.e., life on Earth] is just a tiny part of an overwhelmingly hostile universe. It is even harder to realize that this present universe has evolved from an unspeakably unfamiliar early condition, and faces a future extinction of endless cold or intolerable heat. The more the universe seems comprehensible, the more it also seems pointless.[8]

I fail to share Weinberg's stark, materialistic viewpoint that humanity is a farcical accident. Indeed, I believe that humanity is a necessary creative force in the universe. At the very least, a scientific worldview should do nothing to dispel the miraculous fact of the universe's *being* and the way humans assign it a meaning: science has nothing to say (so far) about existence, only about what things there are and how they behave according to laws. Even here it isn't solid. Simply look at the ongoing debate (raging since at least the Pre-Socratic Parmenides) over whether time is real or not, or on whether the future exists or not, or whether space is infinitely divisible or not. We still don't know, vacillating between the same opposing positions of old. We don't even know the nature of the most basic elements of physics, let alone why they exist. What narrow-mindedness then to ignore these most important issues because our science fails to adequately capture them. One might as well say, with Sir Arthur Eddington, that whatever is too small to be captured in a fisherman's net does not exist.

In any case, in the above passage, much depends on what is meant by "comprehensible." Weinberg is thinking purely of understanding via the laws of physics. Like many a modern physicist, he thinks once we have nailed down the details of the elementary particles, we have all the rest taken care of. This is nonsense. Finding a theory of everything, in the sense of superstring theory, say, would not provide an account of meaning and would not resolve the puzzle of existence. There is no feeling of finding home in a theory like this. There is no unseen order according to which it all makes sense. Comprehending the universe means comprehending all that it involves, and that includes humanity and meaning. Comprehending the role of humanity in the universe leads us to the very opposite conclusion to Weinberg, the anti-Copernican one that Roger Penrose stated quite clearly earlier, in chapter 3: a world without humans really is pointless. To think otherwise is simply an artifact of the hubris of today's conception of science.

Weinberg's barren view is not shared by several other great physicists in fact. The very opposite view was espoused by John Wheeler (a colleague of Weinberg's at the University of Texas), who goes even further than Penrose:

Today I think we are beginning to suspect that man is not a tiny cog that doesn't really make much difference to the running of the huge machine, but rather that there is a much more intimate tie between man and the universe than we heretofore suspected! The physical world is in some deep sense tied to the human being.[9]

The universe is not only pointless without us—I would also urge that it is *inconceivable*—you might think it perfectly easy to conceive of a world without humans, but your conception still comes from a subjective standpoint. Human subjectivity provides the engine that makes the universe go. We mutually demand one another. Mankind is in this case positioned at the heart of the mystery of the existence of universe. Wheeler thought it was crazy to try and understand everything from physics alone, as Weinberg tries to do: No man, no meaning. No meaning, no reason.[10] In a very similar vein, Jung wrote, in his memoirs, *Memories, Dreams, and Reflections,*

> [M]an is indispensable for the completion of creation; that, in fact, he himself is the second creator of the world, who alone has given to the world its objective existence— without which, unheard, unseen, silently eating, giving birth, dying, heads nodding through hundreds of millions of years, it would have gone on in the profoundest night of non-being down to its unknown end. Human consciousness created objective existence and meaning, and man found his indispensable place in the great process of being.[11]

The universe is simply not an object unless there is a subject to reflect it as such, bringing chaos into order, potentiality into actuality and objectivity. We are bound together in such a duality, which is precisely where meaning arises.[12] What greater meaning of life could there be than taking on some responsibility in the very creation of the universe?[13]

The universe repays the favor by supplying us with meaning through the termination of life. This might appear less of a miracle than life, to say the least, but it truly is just as miraculous. Mortality is not a necessary truth: it might not have been this way, and we do not contradict ourselves to think otherwise. The narrowing of life also focuses. Moreover, noticing the existence of the world, and its apparent lack of ground, soon brings with it the thought that it didn't have to be. This is an anxiety-provoking idea. As Schopenhauer put it, "The uneasiness which keeps the never-resting clock of metaphysics in motion, is the consciousness that the non-existence of this world is just as possible as its existence." Schopenhauer too linked the very urge to consider the problem of existence with the limit provided by death:

> If our life were endless and painless, it would perhaps occur to no one to ask why the world exists, and is just the kind of world it is; but everything would just be taken as a matter of course.[14]

We often speak of life (or being) as a miracle and death (nonbeing) as its opposing force, something (an evil, perhaps) to be struggled with. This usual polarity can be avoided if we view death through the temporal boundaries and transience it supplies us with as enabling decisions in the face of choices that bring life into the sphere of actuality, and out of the merely possible (or provisional, which, as we have seen, is not life at all). The German novelist Thomas Mann puts this point most beautifully:

What I believe, what I value most, is transitoriness.

But is not transitoriness—the perishableness of life—something very sad? No! It is the very soul of existence. It imparts value, dignity, interest to life. Transitoriness creates time—and "time is the essence." Potentially at least, time is the supreme, most useful gift.

Time is related to—yes, identical with—everything creative and active, with every progress toward a higher goal.

Without transitoriness, without beginning or end, birth or death, there is no time, either. Timelessness—in the sense of time never ending, never beginning—is a stagnant nothing. It is absolutely uninteresting.

Life is possessed by tremendous tenacity. Even so its presence remains conditional, and as it had a beginning, so it will have an end. I believe that life, just for this reason, is exceedingly enhanced in value, in charm.[15]

This rather neatly sums up the credo I have been trying to unpack in this little book; only it is a summing up by one of the greats. Yet Mann was himself simply summing up millennia of the same, not least Seneca himself, as we have seen—Mann's "stagnant nothing" is Seneca's "long tossing about" is Jung's "provisional life."

Similarly, the great essayist (widely regarded to be the originator of that format) Michel de Montaigne wrote a kind of Renaissance self-help guide, himself updating Seneca's work on the shortness of life, entitled "That to Study Philosophy Is to Learn to Die" (1580). In it, he writes,

The end of our race is death; 'tis the necessary object of our aim, which, if it fright us, how is it possible to advance a step without a fit of ague? The remedy the vulgar use is not to think on't; but from what brutish stupidity can they derive so gross a blindness? They must bridle the ass by the tail.

Your death is a part of the order of the universe, 'tis a part of the life of the world.[16]

In Plato's view (as expressed in his *Phaedo* 67e—a dialogue using Socrates's voice, as he is preparing to drink the hemlock), philosophy constituted, first and foremost, a kind of "training for dying" (understood as a separation of soul and body). The reasons look very Buddhistic, for it is the detached, clean manner in which the philosopher lives (or is *supposed* to live according to Plato: no drink, sex, or bodily pleasure). But more importantly, the philosopher already has experience with the eternal Forms, which, rather than the ordinary experience of the senses, are the philosopher's bread and butter. If philosophy is against the body, and death is an immortal soul shedding this body, then we can take his point. But even if we do not accept this demanding and outmoded view, philosophy can still act as a kind of preparation for death by providing us with the mental tools for making sense of death as a good rather than evil force in the world.

I have argued that it is the *limit* imposed by death that is so crucial. It acts like a big flashing neon sign calling us to life. Such limits become most directly observed at a moment of crisis. There are times when we fully realize we stand at a fork in the road, or we feel on the edge of a cliff. The feeling is anxiety, because we know at such moments we are pruning some possibilities away in an irreversible fashion. I have argued that the anxiety is rational because it is a momentous thing. Often this comes at midlife, of course, because we know that we are also at a turning point in life: at best, halfway to the end. At this point, decisions seem to take on a greater magnitude precisely because our options are becoming more limited. Indeed, the very word "crisis" comes from the Greek word for deciding: *krinein*. Yet not to decide is to live in a nonactual situation, in which all possibilities are still laid out. This keeping open of one's options might seem smart, akin to shrewd management of a financial portfolio, but it simply removes one from actuality, one stagnates, and the closer one gets to the end (which cannot be stopped, I suspect, even with the best advances in gerontology), the less one will have really lived. Moreover, one's possibilities are still being pruned by the impersonal advance of time, rather than by will or conscious design. One cultivates nothing like this. One makes no statement. One does not answer the question put to you by the universe, *à la* Jung: who are you?

Life is a miracle, but so is death. Death is where the meaning is born, and death is where growth comes from. Of course, even in orthodox biology death is central to the structure of life in this way. There is a curious biological example showing just how crucial death and some kind of limitation is, as noted by the British ecologist Woodley of Menie.[17] Woodley of Menie (Michael Woodley, the son of the Baron of Menie) is an interesting case, though a highly controversial figure for studying issues of race and intelligence. He has argued that we are getting ever more stupid as a result of an ever easier existence—this is "the Woodley effect," which means the fall of average general intelligence in the West since the Victorian era. Survival is now more or less given. Of course, we might just as well call it the "Schopenhauer effect," since Schopenhauer was effectively making the same point in his remarks about the link between a questioning mindset and pain and suffering.

Woodley gives an example[18] (based on John B. Calhoun's work) in which

> mouse colonies raised in "utopian" conditions—i.e., in which resources were abundant and predation was absent— although initially experiencing a stage of sustained population growth, eventually stopped reproducing and died out. Notably, toward the end of the colonies' existence, the mice exhibited a number of aberrant behaviors, including ... autistic-like ones.[19]

The mice "lost their meaning" through a lack of limitation. They stagnated. He goes on to expand to humans, arguing that "[th]ere is ... evidence that the same process is playing out in modernized human populations today."[20] While somewhat hyperbolic, it is hard to deny that there is a grain of truth to this, and as we cure more and more diseases and make our lives easier and without obstruction, we threaten to stagnate like the mice, with some kind of collapse possible, whether in the form of an extinction of life or an extinction of culture and values.[21] Those who have achieved a certain degree of comfort but started from uncomfortable circumstances know well the truth in this—it is much harder to battle with new ideas and be a creative force when one has all of one's needs met. Some struggle or battle is required—a barrier, even if only in the form of a deadline for a book.

Let me try and put some of these ideas together in a way more related to the earlier themes, as well as distinguishing our approach here from other superficially similar statements about the importance of death for a meaningful life. Firstly, we can view each of us as having a particular possibility structure that we carry around with us, a *space of possibilities* comprising a branching structure of the ways the world (and we ourselves) could be given the appropriate actions. These will differ for each of us, for we are born in different contexts and with different advantages and disadvantages. What is possible for one person might not be possible for another in the sense that there might be no conceivable sequence of acts of will leading there. There is plenty of luck (good and bad) in the structure of one's possibility space. Our decisions in the face of choices (branch points) quite naturally affect our possibility space, closing some possibilities off often on a permanent basis, or enough to render them as good as impossible.

Take as an example a musical case (it could easily be generalized to other choices). Suppose you like two instruments, violin and piano. But you want to be a virtuoso. There will be a point, if you're young and gifted enough, where you could be either a virtuoso violinist or a virtuoso pianist, but let us suppose you cannot be both (a quite reasonable assumption, given the demands of achieving such levels). You choose violin and thereby realize a track in your possibility structure by cutting a branch (virtuoso pianist) along with all of its subsequent possibilities—or at least you would be *damaging* that branch enough that it begins to quickly die: there is a chance to change your mind for a short time, but as time advances, the possibility structure continues to change with the aging process and the finite hard boundary of death asserting themselves.

Now, our decisions clearly affect such possibilities, but the universe keeps track of these, as it must, since they result in physical changes: the world must be consistent with our decisions, altering its own possibility structure as we go.[22] This is the mundane yet miraculous feature discussed in this chapter, namely that we get to play a constructive role in how the universe goes. When you leave a footprint in the snow, you are leaving a footprint in the universe: you can change it. The bigger the footprint, the bigger the change in the structure and evolution of the universe. But the very possibility structure assigned to us is, in the first place, dictated by the hard limit imposed on us by the universe: we are constrained by it, as it is constrained by us.

Without a short life, we do not face such issues of choice and possibility-pruning in the first place. Yet these choices are at the root of a significant life, a life lived freely and with purpose. They are the stuff of meaning. Hence, there is a curious interplay of limit (provided by the universe in the form of decay and death) and possibility, in which we engage in a dance with the universe, each gifting something meaningful to the other. Each gifting meaning itself to the other. This goes far further than Seneca's view of the shortness of life. It isn't merely that it is only short if we waste it. That very shortness is of the essence.

―――――

Let us now make like an Ouroboros and end where we began, with the *I Ching*'s rather mystical statement about the necessity of limitation. Here is the remainder of that opening passage, which I had earlier truncated:

I Ching, Hexagram 60: To become strong, a man's life needs the limitations ordained by duty and voluntarily accepted. The individual attains significance as a free spirit only by surrounding himself with these limitations and by determining for himself what his duty is.[23]

Without choice and decision in the face of choices (i.e., limitation: letting options go in favor of others), there is no freedom to act.

In this brief hexagram of the *I Ching*, we thus find the dialectical resolution of the pair of opposites, *Puer* (freedom) and *Senex* (limit) that formed the linchpin of our discussion, and it sounds almost like Orwellian doublethink:

Freedom is Limitation

With this realization we conclude, hopefully with a deeper appreciation of those parts of life that appear to be obstacles—including what appears to be a short life (ending in permanent death)—but really are essential to a meaningful existence. Indeed, while it is more usual to speak of "the meaning of life," here we have focused on "the meaning of death" as the more important, and indeed more fundamental issue. The answer in this case is that death is itself the source of life's meaning, calling us to really live, to force us to think about what kind of life we want, about who we are, to know ourselves and act in the world accordingly, careful in how we create its future.

NOTES

Epigraph

1. William Steig, *Dominic* (New York: Farrar, Straus, Giroux, 1972), 14.

Preface

1. *I Ching*, Hexagram 60, "Limitation," as quoted in Daryl Sharp, *Jungian Psychology Unplugged* (Toronto: Inner City Books, 1998), 108.

2. See the new translation of Seneca, *On the Shortness of Life*, by James Romm, in *How to Have a Life: An Ancient Guide to Using Our Time Well* (Princeton, NJ: Princeton University Press, 2022).

Chapter 1

1. Seneca, *On the Shortness of Life*, section 1.

2. Much early philosophy was more along the lines of self-help than is present-day philosophy, which rarely aims to teach and improve. It was often concerned with developing character and living a good life (*eudaimonia* in Greek). See Pierre Hadot's excellent book, *Philosophy as a Way of Life*, trans. Michael Chase (Oxford: Blackwell, 1995), which unpacks exactly this self-help aspect through the practical concept of "spiritual exercises" (ancient "life hacks," if you like).

3. For an early account, see Tacitus's *Annals: Books 13–16*, trans. John Jackson, Loeb Classical Library 322 (Cambridge, MA: Harvard University Press, 1937), XV.60ff. A good recent biography of Seneca is Emily Wilson's *Seneca: A Life* (London: Penguin, 2014). James Ker's *The Deaths of Seneca* (Oxford: Oxford University Press, 2013) provides more detail than you probably wanted about his death!

4. Lucretius, *On the Nature of Things*, trans. W.H.D. Rouse, rev. by Martin F. Smith, Loeb Classical Library 181 (Cambridge, MA: Harvard University Press,

1924), book iii, 928. Friedrich Wilhelm Joseph von Schelling (1775–1854) spoke in this regard of a "sadness that sticks to all mortal life casting a veil of melancholy" (*Friedrich Wilhelm Joseph Schelling's Sämmtliche Werke*, ed. K.F.A. Schelling, vol. 7, *Philosophische Untersuchungen über das Wesen der menschlichen Freiheit und die damit zusammenhängenden Gegenstände* [Stuttgart: Cotta, 1860], 399). The German novelist Jean Paul called this feeling "Weltschmerz" in *Selina; oder Über die Unsterblichkeit* (Stuttgart: Cotta, 1827).

5. He gives his own examples of poor ways to spend one's gift of time: "It would be tedious to mention all the different men who have spent the whole of their life over chess or ball or the practice of baking their bodies in the sun" (Seneca, *On the Shortness of Life*, trans. C.D.N. Costa [London: Penguin, 1997], 20). I think Seneca and I would have been good friends. Unless otherwise noted, all subsequent references to Seneca's essay are taken from Romm's translation in *How to Have a Life*.

6. Seneca, *On the Shortness of Life*, trans. Costa, 1.

7. G.W.F. Hegel, *Hegel's Science of Logic*, trans. A. V. Miller (Amherst, NY: Humanity Books, 1999), 129. The claim is not original with Hegel, but he puts it well. Seneca himself expressed much the same idea in his tragedy on Mad Hercules (*Hercules furens*): "the first hour that gave us life took away also an hour" (*Scenecae Tragoediae Venetia* [Aldi et Andreae Soceri, 1517], 3 Chor. 874), as did fellow Roman Marcus Manilius in his *Astronomica* (Leipzig: Teubner, 1915), iv. 16: "As we are born we die, and the end commences with the beginning."

8. William James, *Principles of Psychology* (New York: Henry Holt and Company, 1893), 609.

9. Viktor Zuckerkandl, *Sound and Symbol* (Princeton, NJ: Princeton University Press, 1969), 161.

10. Seneca, *On the Shortness of Life*, trans. Costa, 2.

11. Ibid., section 7.

12. A superb book on death anxiety is Irvin Yalom's *Staring at the Sun: Overcoming the Terror of Death* (New York: John Wiley and Sons Ltd, 2009). Yalom is an example of an *existential psychotherapist*, a relatively new branch of therapy dealing with issues of meaning and meaninglessness and their relation to anxiety.

13. Cited in D. J. Enright, ed., *The Oxford Book of Death* (Oxford: Oxford University Press, 1983), 22.

14. Epicurus, *Letter to Menoeceus*, trans. Robert Drew Hicks, http://classics.mit.edu/Epicurus/menoec.html.

15. Lucretius, *On the Nature of Things*, book iii, vv. 972.

16. Michel Houellebecq Interview, "Writing Is Like Cultivating Parasites in Your Brain," https://www.youtube.com/watch?v=AJI8YPopjgk.

17. Herman Melville, *White-Jacket* (Boston: Simonds, 1850), p. 143.

Chapter 2

1. Leoš Janáček, *The Makropulos Case*, trans. Norman Tucker (Vienna: Universal Edition A.G., 1966).

2. Philip Larkin, "Aubade," *Times Literary Supplement*, December 2, 1977. Ernst Becker argued similarly in his book *The Denial of Death* (New York: Free Space Paperbacks, 1973), where he viewed religion as a kind of "defence mechanism" forming part of our "immortality project," elevating us beyond the merely physical.

3. "The Makropulos Case" is reprinted in Bernard Williams, *Problems of the Self: Philosophical Papers 1956–1972* (Cambridge: Cambridge University Press, 1973), 82–100.

4. As Nietzsche put it, "Your whole life, like a sandglass, will always be reversed and will ever run out again, a long minute of time will elapse until all those conditions out of which you were evolved return in the wheel of the cosmic process. And then you will find every pain and every pleasure, every friend and every enemy, every hope and every error, every blade of grass and every ray of sunshine once more, and the whole fabric of things which make up your life" (*Notes on the Eternal Recurrence*, in *Nietzsche's Complete Works*, ed. Oscar Levy [London: Macmillan, 1991], 16:33–34).

5. Thomas Reid, *Essays on the Intellectual Powers of Man*, ed. Derek R. Brookes (University Park: Pennsylvania State University Press, 2002).

6. The argument against Locke is that the general would be seen to be the same as the officer, and the officer the same as the boy, but the general would not be the same as the boy, which is an absurdity. For more on this, see American philosopher Sydney Shoemaker's excellent piece, "Personal Identity," in *Encyclopedia Britannica*, https://www.britannica.com/topic/personal-identity.

7. Plato, *Phaedo*, trans. C. J. Rowe (Cambridge: Cambridge University Press, 1993), cf. 102a–107a. For more on this issue, see C. J. Ducasse, "Survival as Transmigration," in *Immortality*, ed. Paul Edwards (Amherst, NY: Prometheus, 1997), 194–99.

8. From Tom Templeton, "Holding Back the Years," *The Observer*, September 16, 2007. His mission can be found expressed in his book *Ending Aging: The Rejuvenation Breakthroughs That Could Reverse Human Aging in Our Lifetime* (New York: St. Martin's Griffin, 2008).

9. Telomeres protect the ends of the chromosomes, preventing their deterioration or fusion with other chromosomes—this mechanism lies at the root of so-called clinical immortality, since they control cellular life and death. A brief review is Ewen Callaway's "Telomerase Reverses Ageing Process," *Nature*, November 28, 2010. A nice simple, general introduction to the science of immortality (if a little dated) is Brian Appleyard's *How to Live Forever or Die Trying: On the New Immortality* (New York: Simon and Schuster, 2007).

10. "Curing Ageing and the Consequences: An Interview with Aubrey de Grey," *EMBO Reports* 6 (2005): 198–201.

11. Williams, "Makropulos Case," 100. The TV comedy *The Good Place* (where the "good place" is the afterlife) offers an amusing treatment of some philosophical issues concerning immortality. The penultimate episode, "Patty," concerns precisely the notion of meaninglessness in eternity, and offers those in the afterlife a "way out," to nothingness, which many gladly take.

Chapter 3

1. Taken from a 1989 interview of the English physicist Roger Penrose by Alan Lightman: https://www.aip.org/history-programs/niels-bohr-library/oral-histories/34322.

2. Bill Hicks, *Sane Man* (Rykodisk, 1989).

3. Alan Weisman, *The World Without Us* (London: Virgin Books, 2008).

4. There are several centers of research dealing with the risks of such globally catastrophic events (such risks are labeled "existential"): The Cambridge Centre for the Study of Existential Risk (https://www.cser.ac.uk, founded by my old colleague Huw Price, together with Lord Martin Rees and Skype developer Jaan Tallinn) and the Future of Humanity Institute (https://www.fhi.ox.ac.uk, founded by Nick Bostrom). These websites have a good deal of literature on the nature of such risks and are well worth a look.

5. Stephen Emmott, *Ten Billion* (London: Penguin Press, 2013), 199. Following the book, Emmott seemingly echoed Bill Hicks, speaking of "The Human Plague" (see https://www.youtube.com/watch?v=VUTGQvDQ8xE.)

6. You can learn about this interesting club, whose motto is "May we live long and die out," here: https://vhemt.org/.

7. Paul Ehrlich and Anne Ehrlich, *The Population Bomb* (New York: Ballantine Books, 1968). A good treatment of the deeper history is Charles Mann's book *The Wizard and the Prophet* (New York: Vintage Books, 2019).

8. As described in Samuel Scheffler's Tanner Lectures, in *Death and the Afterlife* (Oxford: Oxford University Press, 2013). A nice BBC Radio 4 program on "Samuel Scheffler on the Afterlife" can be heard at https://www.bbc.co.uk/programmes /b06084l6.

9. P. D. James, *The Children of Men* (London: Faber & Faber, 1992).

10. *Annie Hall*, directed by Woody Allen (United Artists, 1977).

11. William James, *Is Life Worth Living?* (Philadelphia: S. Burns Weston, 1896). The talk was addressed to the Harvard YMCA in 1895—well before the Village People, so I'm pretty sure he didn't do the YMCA dance.

12. See Thomas Nagel, "The Absurd," *Journal of Philosophy* 68, no. 20 (1971): 716–27.

13. From Albert Camus, *The Myth of Sisyphus and Other Essays*, trans. Justin O'Brien (New York: Alfred A. Knopf, 1955), 21 and 28. See also Robert Zaretsky, *A Life Worth Living: Albert Camus and the Quest for Meaning* (Cambridge, MA: Harvard University Press, 2016).

14. See, e.g., Friedrich Nietzsche, *The Gay Science*, ed. Bernard Williams, trans. Josefine Nauckhoff (Cambridge: Cambridge University Press, 2001).

15. Jean-Paul Sartre, *Existentialism Is a Humanism*, trans. Carol Macomber, ed. John Kulka (New Haven, CT: Yale, 2007), p. vii.

16. Scheffler, *Death and the Afterlife*, 44. William James writes, "The greatest use of life is to spend it on something that will outlast it" (Letter to W. Lutoslawski, November 13, 1900, as cited in *The Thought and Character of William James*, ed. P. Barton [Oxford: Oxford University Press, 1935], 237). But, of course, a legacy needs *custodians* to tend it.

17. Lionel Penrose and Roger Penrose, "Impossible Objects: A Special Type of Visual Illusion," *British Journal of Psychology* 49, no. 1 (1958): 31–33. Roger's siblings (two brothers and one sister) are also highly accomplished: a geneticist, a chess grand master, as well as another physicist, famous in his own right. Both Lionel Penrose and his brother (Roger's uncle) Roland were connected to the Bloomsbury group. Roland was a surrealist artist and was married for a time to the photographer Lee Miller, once Man Ray's muse.

18. This viewpoint can be found in Roger Penrose's first book, *The Emperor's New Mind* (Oxford: Oxford University Press, 1989).

19. The details are of course technical, but, roughly, with no standard of size, the universe can be rescaled down to something corresponding to another initial

singularity (and so on ad infinitum). Penrose has written an introductory guide to his views in his book *Cycles of Time* (London: Bodley Head, 2010).

20. Martin Heidegger, *Being and Time*, trans. Joan Stambaugh (New York: SUNY Press, 2010). I'm very reluctant to offer this as suggested further reading: it is notorious for being one of the most impenetrable books ever written. Oh, and he also happened to be a bit of a Nazi sympathizer.

21. Ibid.

22. Ibid. Sartre, in his *Being and Nothingness*, trans. Sarah Richmond (New York: Washington Square Press, 2021), argued that death in fact causes problems for having lives imbued with meaning: it makes them absurd in the way discussed earlier. In this, he was reacting to Heidegger's *Being and Time*, in which he advances a view similar to the one that I'm advocating, about the close bond between meaning and death. Sartre defends a view of meaning through creativity, while Heidegger gains it from projects carried out in conditions of finitude.

Chapter 4

1. Philip Larkin, "Reference Back," in *The Whitsun Weddings* (London: Faber Poetry, 2010), 47.

2. And there is a good biological basis for this kind of preferential treatment of kin. See Robert Sapolsky's masterful (and highly amusing) lectures online for the reasons: "Human Behavioral Biology (Robert Sapolsky) 25 lectures," https://www.youtube.com/playlist?list=PL150326949691B199. Sometimes browsing YouTube is *not* a waste of time. I feel sure Seneca would approve.

3. Monkey on a pig always wins, of course.

4. Seneca, *On the Shortness of Life*, section 9.

5. An old colleague at the University of Leeds, Seiriol Morgan, had a sign on his office: "The Institute for Applied Akrasia," which I always wished I'd thought of!

6. Incidentally, you can find a good example of the kind of temporal myopia discussed here in that other Homer: Homer Simpson. In the episode "Money-Bart" (directed by Nancy Kruse, written by Tim Long, aired October 10, 2010, Fox), Homer responds to Marge's worries about the children by saying, "That's a problem for future Homer! Man, I don't envy that guy!" After which he pours a bottle of vodka in a jar of mayonnaise and downs the whole thing! Hal Herschfeld, whom we will mention in a moment, has found another great example in *Seinfeld* ("The Glasses," directed by T. Cherones, written by T. Gammill and M. Pross, aired September 30, 1993, Columbia Pictures Television): "I never get enough sleep. I stay

up late at night, 'cause I'm Night Guy. [*Laughter*] Night Guy wants to stay up late. What about getting up after five hours sleep? Oh, that's Morning Guy's problem. That's not my problem, I'm Night Guy. I stay up as late as I want. So you get up in the morning, you yawn, you're exhausted, groggy, ooh I hate that Night Guy! See, Night Guy always screws Morning Guy. There's nothing Morning Guy can do. The only thing Morning Guy can do is try and oversleep often enough so that Day Guy loses his job and Night Guy has no money to go out anymore."

7. Derek Parfit, *Reasons and Persons* (Oxford: Oxford University Press, 1988), 313.

8. Hal Hershfield's original paper is "Saving for the Future Self: Neural Measures of Future Self-Continuity Predict Temporal Discounting," *Social Cognitive and Affective Neuroscience* 4, no. 1 (2009): 85–92. A TED talk ("How Can We Help Our Future Selves?") makes many of the same points in a simpler format: https://www.youtube.com/watch?v=tJotBbd7MwQ.

9. Parfit, *Reasons and Persons*, 281.

10. If you would like to learn more, however, go read Bohm's book (coauthored with Basil Hiley): *The Undivided Universe: An Ontological Interpretation of Quantum Theory* (London: Routledge, 1993).

11. The original theory, based on the role of mental time travel in survival (i.e., evolutionary advantage), is due to the Estonian psychologist Endel Tulving, as presented in his book *Elements of Episodic Memory* (Oxford: Oxford University Press, 1985). A useful discussion is Dan Falk's *In Search of Time* (Manhattan: St Martins, Griffin, 2010).

12. See Jean-Louis van Gelder, Hal Hershfield, and Loren Nordgren, "Vividness of the Future Self Predicts Delinquency," *Psychological Science* 24, no. 6 (2013): 974–80. The authors speak of "making friends" with your future self. That's one way of approaching it, and it seems to have fairly decent results. I favor a more natural approach, which is to view the relation as *identity* rather than friendship, unity rather than multiplicity. You probably care somewhat less about your friends than yourself, so identity is a far stronger relation.

13. See Walter Mischel, *The Marshmallow Test: Understanding Self-Control and How to Master It* (London: Corgie Adult, 2015).

14. Seneca, *On the Shortness of Life*, section 3.

15. Jolande Jacobi, *The Way of Individuation* (New York: Plume, 1983), 26.

16. An excellent discussion of this feature of midlife is Kieran Setiya's *Midlife: A Philosophical Guide* (Princeton, NJ: Princeton University Press, 2017).

17. "Enjoy Yourself (It's Later Than You Think)," music by Herb Magidson, words by Carl Sigman, 1948 (renewed), Magidson Bernhardt Music and Music

Sales Corporation. All rights for Bernhardt Music administered by WC Music Corp. All rights reserved. Used by permission of Alfred Music. My personal favorite version appears in Woody Allen's movie *Everyone Says I Love You*, but other great versions include The Specials' and Louis Prima's.

Chapter 5

1. Jalal ad-Din Muhammad Rumi, *Rumi: In the Arms of the Beloved*, trans. Jonathan Star, (London: Penguin, 2008), 170.

2. Sartre, *Existentialism Is a Humanism*, 37.

3. Of course, I acknowledge that these procedures will differ from person to person and context to context. Often someone simply will not have the resources another has, and so will have to follow a different set of steps to create the desired future. Moreover, I take it to be obvious that I do not mean that we have control over the universe in all its aspects! Just a great deal of those local to you, and certainly more than is often supposed. Most importantly, sometimes the finite boundary of death will simply rule many things out. But then, these are not really branches of possibility in the universe at all, and not fit for pruning, but mere phantasms. Likewise, since we share a common universe, someone else's carvings can take away some of your own creative possibilities, requiring adaptation or abandoning as the case may be.

4. One can imagine this *not* being the case, of course, say if one were told that one would have to undergo an operation that would result in a complete reconfiguration of one's mind to such an extent that one would not feel such an enduring self—say, if you were given an intense electric shock treatment. But that would be a kind of termination. Or perhaps there is the discovery of the genes underlying Alzheimer's that will with certainty lead to a disconnection in selfhood—we already know of several such genes. Then, perhaps, why bother? But so long as you are operating under ordinary circumstances, you have every reason to put in the work now because *you* will be the one enjoying the fruits of that labor.

5. In his book *The Time Cure* (Hoboken, NJ: Jossey-Bass, 2012), Philip Zimbardo (he of the Stanford Prison Experiment—though his work on the so-called time cure is far superior in my opinion) treats the distribution problem quite literally, dividing our temporal stance (relative to the present moment we always experience ourselves as occupying) into five possible perspectives (the original research paper is "Putting Time in Perspective: A Valid, Reliable Individual-Differences Metric," *Journal of Personality and Social Psychology* 77, no. 6 [1999]: 1271–88), which he coauthored with his student John Boyd):

1. Past-positive people focus on the "good old days." They may keep scrapbooks, collect photos, and look forward to celebrating traditional holidays.

2. Past-negative people focus on all the things that went wrong in the past: "It doesn't matter what I do, my life will never change."

3. Present-hedonistic people live in the moment: seeking pleasure, novelty, and sensation, and avoiding pain.

4. Present-fatalistic people feel that decisions are moot because predetermined fate plays the guiding role in life: "What will be, will be."

5. Future-oriented people plan for the future and trust that their decision will work out.

Another perspective was added later:

6. Transcendental-future-oriented people believe that life after death is more important than the life they are living. They may invest heavily in the afterlife during their current lifetime.

The latter category includes the Egyptians preparing their way with pyramids, but we can find it in the lives of many religious people, who are likewise preparing for judgment and so living with that in mind. More mundanely, perhaps, we can imagine giving some thought to one's legacy, including what one will leave for one's children. The theory of Zimbardo then essentially traces all manner of psychological (and ultimately physical) problems to the dominance of one or other of these perspectives. As with Seneca, it is all a matter of balance: too much of one or the other leads to problems. But of course the problem is, how do we get better at some desirable component, and cut the other negative ones out? Knowing which one is half the battle, but the hardest part is the active and authentic molding.

6. Einstein's remark comes from a letter he penned to the widow of his recently deceased friend, Michele Besso. Einstein to Mrs. Besso, March 15, 1955, in *Albert Einstein, Michele Besso: Correspondence: 1903–1955,* ed. Pierre Speziali (Paris: Herman, 1979), 537–38. Einstein wanted to offer some comfort by pointing out that according to his theory of relativity, Besso and his wife were still together in the universe, since past, present, and future exist with the same reality status: they were simply in different space-time locations, functioning much like our (indexical) word "here." Viewed in this way, we might interpret Einstein's remark as another kind of immortality, for we exist eternally in this way.

7. See Sam Mowe, "Tibetan Monks Found Chanting Text by Oxford Philosopher," *Tricycle: The Buddhist Review,* September 13, 2011. Note the link here to the

unimportance of death, for if relationship to the future self is not so important, then the disconnection of that relation (through death) is not so important either. This is another affinity with Buddhism, and another reason I fail to share the viewpoint, for it advocates a dissolving of life into the boundless.

8. John Earman, "Reassessing the Prospects for a Growing Block Model of the Universe," *International Studies in the Philosophy of Science* 22, no. 2 (2008): 135–64.

9. See William James, *The Meaning of Truth: A Sequel to "Pragmatism"* (New York and London: Longmans, Green, 1909), 226.

10. James expresses these views in his 1884 essay "The Dilemma of Determinism," reprinted in *The Will to Believe and Other Essays in Popular Philosophy* (Cambridge: Cambridge University Press, 2014), 145–83. By way of a flashback to the previous chapter, James in his later years put life after death in this category of *beyond evidence* and therefore suitable for filling in with whatever makes one's world feel a little better. He chose to believe that we are immortal. See his 1897 Ingersoll Lecture "Immortality" at https//www.hds.harvardlibrary/ingersoll/18971ec—the Ingersoll series was devoted to the topic of immortality. Jung also believed that some sense of immortality was a kind of rational need (the need to continue in life) possessed by all humans.

11. Sartre, *Being and Nothingness*, 87ff.

12. Stefan Kanfer, ed., *The Essential Groucho: Writings by, for, and about Groucho Marx* (London: Penguin, 2008), 151.

13. C. J. Jung, *Memories, Dreams, and Reflections*, trans. Richard and Clara Winston (New York: Vintage Books, 1989), 362.

14. I think the controversial, conservative philosopher Roger Scruton nicely exemplified this—however unpopular this opinion might be, I happen to be a fan. He had a classic troubled childhood, with distant parents unable to reflect back to him the safety required, thus depriving him of a notion of *home*. He made this search for home the archstone of his philosophy and his way of living. So far as I can tell, though he obviously knew that his childhood led to this search—in his memoirs, *Gentle Regrets: Thoughts from a Life* (London: Continuum, 2006), he is very perceptive about the split that occurred in his youth in which he constructed a false self to bear the brunt of a harsh reality—he never looked more deeply to consider that in choosing to give himself what he never had by way of home (in his case, a rather regal existence among the gentry, which his father so detested), his childhood (and his parents) were still controlling his decisions, so that he had never really grown up. I'm sure the same could be said of a great many of my own actions (including writing a book such a this).

15. The shunning of the power of dreams among contemporary scientists, as with many things (of a nonmaterialist nature) currently believed to be amusing relics of a bygone era, belies an inability to see what is in front of one's face. The waking brain is suffused with material, churning out meaning all the time. To think that this should suddenly cease during sleep, while the brain scrambles itself, only to instantaneously reassemble on waking, is simply absurd. Those who ignore the content of their dreams are missing out on a great deal of potentially valuable information. Fortunately, this neglect is changing somewhat: see, e.g., Mark Solms's book *The Hidden Spring: A Journey to the Source of Consciousness* (London: Profile Trade, 2021).

16. One of many excellent aphorisms to be found in Arthur Schopenhauer, *The Wisdom of Life and Counsels and Maxims*, trans. T. Bailey Saunders (New York: Prometheus Books, 1995).

17. William Shakespeare, *As You Like It* (New York: Simon and Schuster, 2011), act 2, scene 8.

Chapter 6

1. *Love and Death*, written and directed by Woody Allen, produced by Charles H. Joffe (MGM/UA, 1975).

2. Marie-Louise von Franz, *The Problem of the Puer Aeternus* (Toronto: Inner City Books, 2000), 8.

3. Jung mentions the idea in *The Psychology of Kundalini Yoga*, ed. Sonu Shamdasani (Princeton, NJ: Princeton University Press, 2012), 28. Baynes's essay "The Provisional Life" was reprinted as chapter 4 of *Analytical Psychology and the English Mind: And Other Papers* (London: Routledge, 2016), 61–76.

4. Seneca, *Ad Lucilium Epistulae Morales*, ed. Richard M. Gummere, 3 vols., Loeb Classical Library 75–77 (Cambridge, MA: Harvard University Press, 1917–25).

5. Von Franz, *Puer Aeternus*, 1–2.

6. Ibid., 8.

7. C. G. Jung, *Visions: Notes of the Seminar Given in 1930–1934*, ed. Claire Douglas (Princeton, NJ: Princeton University Press, 1997), 1147.

8. In more modern literature, the novelist Michel Houellebecq's protagonists often have the characteristics of *Puers*: a listless life that fails to fill a void. I can think of no better introduction to this phenomenon than his works.

9. It is important to state that this shadow is not necessarily a bad object: it is simply the material that one does not like about oneself. This could include what

we would ordinarily consider to be *good* qualities, such as drive, potency, creativity, and so on, which have been expunged (not always consciously) as a result of some conflict or trauma (such as not wishing to be like a particular parent, and so not allowing such qualities to make any appearance in one's surface, visible self). One cannot really do this on a permanent basis, and such qualities will often attempt to make themselves seen, often surprising the surface self, in acting out, strange dreams, strange associations, or noticing that certain things in the world seem to be taking on symbolic meaning, and so on.

10. Von Franz, *Puer Aeternus*, 157.

11. Albert Camus, *The Myth of Sisyphus*, trans. Justin O'Brien (London: Hamish Hamilton, 1955).

12. This is of course one of the basic ideas behind mindfulness practice. This does, however, not quite work in Jung's sense, since there is still something thoroughly self-absorbed about the *doing* of meditation, regardless of the fact that the ultimate goal is to lose oneself. There is still something "out of touch with mundane reality" here. Something more Godlike than human.

13. Marcel Proust, *In Search of Lost Time: The Guermantes Way*, trans. Mark Treharne (London: Penguin Classics, 2005), 575.

14. Camus, *Myth of Sisyphus*.

15. There is a rumor, probably apocryphal, that the most famous nonfictional rake, Giacomo Casanova, had a hand in writing the libretto. Casanova was friends with the librettist, Lorenzo da Ponte. And Mozart and Casanova certainly lived in Prague at the same time. Perhaps one day some concrete evidence will turn up: I hope it is true!

16. Otto Rank, *The Don Juan Legend*, trans. David G. Winter (Princeton, NJ: Princeton University Press, 2016).

17. See Barbara Kraft's memoir *Anaïs Nin: The Last Days* (Los Angeles: Sky Blue Press, 2011) for a clear, insightful discussion of these aspects: "The golden crown fell out in clumps on the bathroom floor, and she was attached, through an incision on her right side, to a series of bags that contained the bilious, acidic fluids draining from her broken body. These years of pain and suffering rendered her a mortal being, made of flesh and bones and blood" (from the preface).

18. Rank, *Don Juan Legend*, 21.

19. It is also a useful exercise to try and identify which of these characteristics describe you, and whether you have experienced any swings from one pole to the other, and why. Do you need to move in the other direction? Have you overcorrected?

20. See David John Tacey, "James Hillman: The Unmaking of a Psychologist Part Two: The Problem of the Puer," *Journal of Analytical Psychology* 59, no. 4 (2014): 486–502.

21. James Hillman, *James Hillman: Senex & Puer*, Seminar, April 16–18, 2010, California (Depth Video, 2010), DVD.

22. Tacey, "James Hillman," 486.

23. Ibid., 493.

24. In his *Modern Man in Search of a Soul* (London: Routledge, 2001), 114, Jung also makes the following highly astute remark in this regard: "To the psychotherapist an old man who cannot bid farewell to life appears as feeble and sickly as a young man who is unable to embrace it. And as a matter of fact, it is in many cases a question of the self-same infantile greediness, the same fear, the same defiance and wilfulness, in the one as in the other."

25. Billy Joel, "Vienna," recorded September 29, 1977, on *The Stranger*, Columbia Records.

26. The psychoanalyst Dan Kiley recast this problem in terms of Peter Pan and presents it as his own invention; see his book *The Peter Pan Syndrome: Men Who Have Never Grown Up* (New York: Dodd Mead, 1983). Yet the concept is an old one, as we have seen. Interestingly, the Lost Boys from Peter Pan eventually grow up and escape Peter Pan's orbit by getting jobs (bankers, office workers, judges, and so on). The "Lost Boys" name was used as the title of a rather good vampire film from 1987. The similarities between *Puers* and vampires should by now be clear: neither will grow up. The subtitle to J. M. Barrie's first Peter Pan novel was, of course, "The Boy Who Wouldn't Grow Up."

Chapter 7

1. Dave Asprey, *Super Human* (New York: Harper Wave, 2019), 232.

2. Jacobi, *Way of Individuation*, 131.

3. Ibid., 32.

4. Jean Arundale, *Identity, Narcissism, and the Other: Object Relations and Their Obstacles* (London: Karnac Books, 2017), 37.

5. Asprey even produced a book implicating the next generation in this disorder: *The Better Baby Book: How to Have a Healthier, Smarter, Happier Baby* (New York: John Wiley & Sons, 2013). I might note that Asprey also supports the "acoustic wave therapy" approach to erectile dysfunction to make these poor "superbabies," not once allowing that most such dysfunction is not physical, but yet another example

of anxiety caused by exactly the kind of perfect, zero-weakness image he promotes. A fair bit of the science behind Asprey's brand relates to Aubrey de Grey's book *The Mitochondrial Free Radical Theory of Ageing* (Austin, TX: R. G. Landes Co, 1999). They are clearly fellow travelers, and I might also add that Asprey boasts of having "had stem cells injected pretty much all over my body in multiple countries," including into his brain: see Dave Asprey, "How Adult Stem Cells Can Help Stop Pain and Reverse Aging," https://www.daveasprey.com/how-adult-stem-cells-can-help-stop-pain-and-reverse-aging/. I let you decide whether this is pathological or not. Note, I am not saying that these interventions do not work: they might well. It is a question of the valuation and usage of one's time. In this case, assuming these methods work, the extension of one's time is occupying that time with no deeper purpose. As the great American essayist Ralph Waldo Emerson put it, "It is not length of life, but depth of life" (Harold Bloom, ed., *Ralph Waldo Emerson: Collected Poems and Translations* [New York: Library of America, 1994], 425).

6. Daryl Sharp, *Jung Lexicon: A Primer of Terms and Concepts* (Toronto: Inner City Books, 1991), 66.

7. Ibid.

8. Worse still: one can try to live up to it and damage the world, in the style of a dictator! This points to a curious aspect of the "sculpture" view of the future, which is that it has been the case that those who appear to implicitly accept this idea (which is correlated with narcissism: a sense that one can control anything and do anything) often implement it all too well, and with devastating consequences.

9. The Cluster B section of the *Diagnostic and Statistical Manual of Mental Disorders*, 5th ed. (DSM-5) (Washington, DC: American Psychiatric Association, 2013) comprises the borderline, histrionic, antisocial, and narcissistic personality disorders that often involve difficulties regulating the emotions, but in which the triggers for disregulation are often related to mismatches between some idealized, perfect vision of reality (projections, which can include projections onto themselves: the false self) and reality itself (which corresponds to a failed projection). Suicides are common in these reality-distortion disorders as a result of both the feeling of unreality (the lack of a real self) and the failure to achieve the perfect vision (which generates a kind of shame). If not suicide, then the offending reality must be eliminated through a process called "splitting," a defense mechanism to maintain the integrity of the fortress of I. See Otto Kernberg's *Borderline Conditions and Pathological Narcissism* (Lanham, MD: Rowan & Littlefield, 1995) for more details.

10. Ovid, *Metamorphosis*, trans. Anthony Kline, https://ovid.lib.virginia.edu/trans/Ovhome.htm.

11. Ibid., book iii, 402–36.

12. James Hollis, *Hauntings: Dispelling the Ghosts Who Ruin Our Lives* (Asheville, NC: Chiron Publications, 2013).

13. C. J. Jung, *Psychology and Alchemy*, trans. R.F.C. Hull (London: Routledge, 1980), para. 152.

14. One can find an interesting variant of this shadow phenomenon in the so-called nice guy syndrome, in which all bad feelings, all selfishness, and so on are hidden (not eliminated: *hidden*). Of course, "nice guys" are usually very far from it: shady, dishonest, and inauthentic. Their very "perfectness" is an imperfection that is easily homed in on and found to be wanting. The niceness is propped up by a very ugly shadow, much like Dorian Gray's grotesque attic-bound portrait. One should let some of these more grotesque parts of oneself see the light of day, to become part of one's conscious outerwear, lest they stay invisible and assert control from the attic.

15. In Jung's words, "The needful thing is not to 'know' the truth but to experience it. Not to have an intellectual conception of things, but to find our way to the inner, perhaps wordless, irrational experiences—that is the heart of the problem" (*The Symbolic Life*, trans. R.F.C. Hull [Princeton, NJ: Princeton University Press, 1977], 558).

16. It might not be a small way. The so-called free will theorem of mathematicians John Conway and Simon Kochen suggests a universe radically open to our interventions. As they put it, "Theodore Roosevelt's decision to build the Panama Canal shows that free will moves mountains, which implies, by general relativity, that even the curvature of space is not determined. The stage is still being built while the show goes on" ("The Free Will Theorem," *Foundations of Physics* 36, no. 10 [2006]: 1441–73).

17. Jacobi, *Way of Individuation*, 102.

18. C. J. Jung, *Symbols of Transformation*, trans. R.F.C. Hall (Princeton, NJ: Princeton University Press, 1967), 617.

19. Von Franz, *Puer Aeternus*, 156.

20. There is some irony in my writing the above, for, truth be told, I am (or was: I'm improving a little …) the worst offender. I confess to still using some of these Bulletproof and related products to fuel my ego. I hope I am doing this in a psychologically healthy manner! My bulletproofing was certainly borderline narcissistic in

the true sense, rendering me so bulletproof as to be inhuman. I suspect Asprey and his bulletproof brigade share my old drive toward inhumanity. Even the terminology of "hacking" bespeaks a view of the body and of life as machine-like. I thought this was a good achievement too, being a *machine* rather than human: better than human = transhuman!

21. Indeed, there is a general tendency to bulletproof our children from a young age, cocooning them from any and all potential mishaps. Of course, all this does is cocoon them from life and experience—and thus meaning. Is it any wonder we have an anxiety epidemic among our kids?

Chapter 8

1. Thich Nhat Hanh, *The Miracle of Mindfulness* (New York: Random House, 1975), 12.

2. Interestingly, Jung was himself against the importing of non-Western traditions into the Western world. Yoga and so on were built for psychic structures outside of our ways. Yet many Westerners view such traditions as offering some kind of salvation, which is an impossibility according to Jung: the search should take place within their own sphere of living.

3. Jacobi, *Way of Individuation*, 19.

4. Foster Wallace could not find it in himself to accept that his earlier work (especially *Infinite Jest*) was his best, committing suicide at forty-six.

5. As quoted in L. Hoffmann, *Postirony: The Nonfictional Literature of David Foster Wallace and Dave Eggers* (Bielefeld: Transcript Verlag, 2016), 171.

6. See Peter Bergmann, "8 Things the Mushroom Told Terence McKenna," April 30, 2016, http://www.mckennite.com/articles/voice.

7. Seneca, *On the Shortness of Life*, section 19.

8. Steven Weinberg, *The First Three Minutes: A Modern View of the Origin of the Universe* (New York: Basic Books, 1993), 154.

9. John Wheeler, interview by Florence Helitzer, *Intellectual Digest*, June 1973, 32.

10. John Wheeler wrote of this quest to understand why the universe exists (one he undertook in his later years) that "I am not 'I' unless I continue to hammer at that nut.... Stop and I become a shrunken old man. Continue and I have a gleam in my eye." See Amanda Gefter, "Haunted by His Brother, He Revolutionized Physics," *Nautilus*, January 10, 2014, https://nautil.us/haunted-by-his-brother -he-revolutionized-physics-rp-7783/. Here is a *Puer*'s quest if ever there was one,

NOTES TO CHAPTER 8 111

much like Parsifal's quest for the Holy Grail, that has the power to enliven a senexian dotage. It is perhaps no surprise that Wheeler's cosmological theories involve cycles of time (eternal recurrence), leading to a kind of immortality in which every death is matched by a rebirth—much like the Ouroboros that, as Jung writes, "slays himself and brings himself to life, fertilizes himself and gives birth to himself" (*Collected Works*, trans. Gerhard Adler and R.F.C. Hull, vol. 14, *Mysterium Coniunctionis* [Princeton, NJ: Princeton University Press, 1977], para. 513).

11. Jung, *Memories, Dreams, and Reflections*, 255–56.

12. In this way, the account of meaning presented in this book stands in stark contrast to the orthodoxy that we find in, e.g., Robert Nozick's *The Examined Life* (New York: Simon and Schuster, 1989)—this account was based on Victor Frankl's account rooted in his Auschwitz experiences (presented in *Man's Search for Meaning*, trans. Harold Kushner [Boston: Beacon Press, 1959]). On these accounts, meaning comes from *transcending* the limitations of the everyday world. Here, I argue that meaning is in the world, an *immanent* feature, there for anyone with sufficient will and consciousness.

13. We could perhaps take this further. As already mentioned, Plato introduced us to the character of the demiurge. What this is, essentially, is a kind of god (though a somewhat lowly one) who is able to organize matter in the universe. This was a divine craftsman, however, that was able to sculpt this orderly cosmos we find ourselves in. Now here's the crazy part: you are able to do exactly this, albeit limited to a small scale, mostly as a result of our constitution. You can mold this universe according to your will. This is mostly trivial because we forget what power we have: we are in a sense all demiurges. We're all divine craftsmen, with the capability (given obvious constraints having to do with laws of nature, which also constrained Plato's demiurge) of choosing how we would like our little bit of the universe to be. (There's a whole other component to Plato's tale, having to do with the demiurge trying to make a realm of eternal forms concrete, and doing so imperfectly, among other things. Read Carl Séan O'Brien's *The Demiurge in Ancient Thought* [Cambridge: Cambridge University Press, 2015] for more details.) The French philosopher Henri Bergson spoke along these same lines of the universe as "a machine for the making of gods" (*The Two Sources of Morality and Religion*, trans. R. Ashley Aura [Notre Dame, IN: University of Notre Dame Press, 1977], 317).

14. Arthur Schopenhauer, *The World as Will and Representation*, trans. R. H. Haldane and J. Kemp (London: Trübner & Company, 1886), 2:360, 361.

15. Thomas Mann, "Life Grows in the Soil of Time," from a *This I Believe* radio broadcast. You can listen to the original broadcast at https://thisibelieve.org/essay

/16783/. These essays were supposed to offer a kind of near-tweet-sized credo of great thinkers' core beliefs—I have abbreviated a little here.

16. Michel de Montaigne, "That to Philosophize Is to Learn How to Die," in *Works of Michel de Montaigne*, ed. W. Hazlitt (New York: Hurd and Houghton, 1864), 121–44.

17. See Grégoir Canlorbe, "A Conversation with Michael A. Woodley of Menie, Yr.," *Psych* 1, no. 1 (2019): 207–19. Also: Edward Dutton and Woodley of Menie's *At Our Wit's End: Why We're Becoming Less Intelligent and What It Means for the Future* (Exeter: Imprint Academic, 2018).

18. I have Harald Atmanspacher to thank for drawing my attention to this example.

19. Canlorbe, "Conversation with Michael A. Woodley," 219.

20. Ibid.

21. Roger Scruton penned many a provocative book arguing that this latter event is already well underway—see, e.g., his *Soul of the World* (Princeton, NJ: Princeton University Press, 2014) or *Modern Culture* (London: Bloomsbury Publishing, 2006).

22. Indeed, I believe it is entirely possible that some aspects of the flow of time are built in this way, by the changing possibility structure that we are involved in.

23. *I Ching*, Hexagram 60, "Limitation," 108.

INDEX

Absurdity, 21

Akrasia, 31

Allen, Woody, 19

Arundale, Jean, 71

Asprey, Dave, 70

Authenticity, xii, 26, 57, 63, 72

Bad faith, 48

Biohacking, 110n20

Bohm, David, 34

Calhoun, John, 90

Camus, Albert, 63

Child prodigies, 74

Creation, 85

Crisis, 89

de Grey, Aubrey, 14

Death anxiety, 7

Delayed gratification, 72–73

Demiurge, 111n13

Don Juan, 64

Dysmorphia, 72, 73–74

Emerson, Ralph Waldo, 108n5

Epicurus, 7

Eudaimonia, 29, 95n2 (chap. 1)

Existentialism, 22

FOMO (fear of missing out), 10

Foster Wallace, David, 81

Hegel, Georg, 96n7

Heidegger, Martin, 26

Herschfeld, Hal, 100n6

Hillman, James, 66

Hollis, James, 75

Houellebecq, Michel, 8

I Ching, xi, 92

Individuation, 49

Jacobi, Jolande, 39, 70

James, William, 21

Jung, Carl Gustav, 42, 50–52, 56,
     58–59, 60, 61, 64, 75, 78, 81,
     104, 110

Kiley, Dan, 107n26

Locke, John, 12

Lucretius, 8

The Makropulos Case, 10
Manilius, Manilius, 96n7
Mann, Thomas, 86–87
Marshmallow Test, 37
Meaning, 22
Meditation, 77
Melville, Herman, 9
Mid-life Crisis, 39
Montaigne, Michel de, 87–88
Myth of Narcissus, 74

Nagel, Thomas, 21

Ouroboros, 92

Parfit, Derek, 31–33, 36, 42, 45, 47
Parsifal, 111n10
Penrose, Roger, 25, 84
Peter Pan, 68
Platonism, 75
Proust, Marcel, 62–63
Puer et Senex, 41, 53, 65, 66, 68,
    110–111n10

Rank, Otto, 64

Sartre, Jean-Paul, 48–49
Scheffler, Samuel, 17
Schopenhauer, Arthur, 52–53
Scruton, Roger, 112n21
Seneca, Lucius Annaeus, 1–3, 6, 29–30,
    96n7
Shadow, 51, 60, 64, 65, 71, 75, 76
Sharp, Daryl, 73
Sisyphus, 60

Tacey, David, 66, 67

von Franz, Marie Louis, 57–58, 60,
    65–67, 78–79

Weinberg, Steven, 83
Wheeler, John, 84–85
Williams, Bernard, 12
Woodley of Menie, Michael, 89

Zimbardo, Philip, 102n5

A NOTE ON THE TYPE

This book has been composed in Arno, an Old-style serif typeface in the classic Venetian tradition, designed by Robert Slimbach at Adobe.